Stolen Inheritance

How the Vulnerable Lose Their Estates —and What Families Can Do

Michael Hackard

Elder Legacy Press

Stolen Inheritance: How the Vulnerable Lose Their Estates—and What Families Can Do

Published by Elder Legacy Press, Mather, California.

ISBN: 979-8-9949360-3-0

Names: Hackard, Michael, author.

Title: Stolen inheritance : how the vulnerable lose their estates -- and what families can do / Michael Hackard.

Description: [First edition]. | Mather, California : Elder Legacy Press, [2026]

Identifiers: ISBN: 9798994936030 (paperback) | 9798994936047 (ebook)

Subjects: LCSH: Inheritance and succession--United States. | Inheritance and succession--California. | Undue influence--United States. | Wills--United States. | Older people--Abuse of--United States--Prevention. | Estate planning--United States. | Claims against decedents' estates--United States. | Probate law and practice--United States. | Decedents' estates--United States--Trial practice. | Finance, Personal--United States. | Financial security--United States. | Older people--Legal status, laws, etc.--United States. | Older people--Legal status, laws, etc.--California. | Legal assistance to older people--United States. | Trusts and trustees--Professional ethics--United States. | Dementia--Patients--Legal status, laws, etc.--United States. | LCGFT: Law for laypersons. | BISAC: LAW / Estates & Trusts. | LAW / Elder Law. | FAMILY & RELATIONSHIPS / Eldercare.

Classification: LCC: KF753 .H332 2026 | DDC: 346.7305/2--dc23

Library of Congress Control Number: 2026912731

Elder Legacy Press
10640 Mather Boulevard
Mather, California 95655

elderlegacypress.com

To my generation, and to the children who carry us—the ones who notice, who ask, who do not look away.

Contents

Author's Note ix

Introduction xi

Chapter 1 1
When It Isn't Alzheimer's

Chapter 2 7
When the Stranger Moves In

Chapter 3 16
The People Who Made It Possible

Chapter 4 25
The Envelope That Looked Like Nothing

Chapter 5 35
The First Thirty Days

Chapter 6 45
Through the Screen

Chapter 7 57
The Structure That Starts the War

Chapter 8 67
What the Record Remembers

Chapter 9 75
The Window

Chapter 10 83
How Cases End: Three Mediations

Chapter 11 94
The Justice Gap

Appendix: Questions And Answers 103

Appendix: For Families 121

Glossary 127

Resources 131

Notes On Sources 133

Author's Note

This book is drawn from fifty years of California trust and estate litigation. Sacramento. The Bay Area—San Francisco, Piedmont, Berkeley, Tiburon, Napa. Los Angeles. Orange County. San Diego. The Central Coast.

It is not a legal manual. California statutes appear in the endnotes, where they belong. It is not a memoir of a career, though the career is the source of every case in these pages.

Most of the cases are anonymized. Names, dates, locations, and identifying facts have been changed or omitted to protect the families involved. The underlying patterns—the timelines, the mechanisms, the legal postures—are unchanged.

Two cases are identified by name because they are part of the public record: the estate of United States Senator Dianne Feinstein and her late husband Richard Blum; and the estate of the actor Robin Williams and his widow Susan Schneider. These matters were litigated in open court or resolved through public proceedings, and the public record carries the same patterns that private files carry.

California provides some of the strongest elder financial abuse protections in the United States. The relevant framework includes Welfare and Institutions Code § 15610.30, defining elder financial abuse; Welfare and Institutions Code § 15610.70, the four-factor test for undue influence; Probate Code § 21380, the presumption that certain donative transfers are the product of undue influence; Probate Code § 850, the statutory vehicle for recovering property wrongfully transferred; Welfare and Institutions Code § 15657.7, the four-year limitations window for financial elder abuse claims; Probate Code § 16061.7, the one-hundred-twenty-day window for contesting a trust after statutory notice; and Code of Civil Procedure § 366.3, the one-year window for claims arising from a promise to inherit.

The legal framework is California-specific. The human story is not. Adult children in every state recognize the sequence by the end of the first chapter.

Introduction

The call comes after the funeral. It almost always does.

They waited until the service was over. Until the relatives had flown back. Until the casseroles stopped arriving. Somewhere in that quiet, the adult child sat down with the trust document and read it carefully, a second time, because the first time didn't make sense.

Then they called the trustee. Usually a sibling. Sometimes a stepmother. Occasionally a stranger whose name they had never heard before their father died.

They got nothing. No accounting. No timeline. No copy of the trust they had been told for years would provide for them.

That is when they call me.

I have taken that call for fifty years.

The Pattern

A vulnerable person. Someone with access. A document signed during a window—weeks, days, sometimes hours—when the person signing could not fully understand what it did.

Then the funeral. Then the call.

The vulnerability takes many forms. Alzheimer's disease. Vascular dementia from a silent stroke. Lewy body dementia, often undiagnosed until autopsy. Alcohol-related cognitive decline. Post-surgical confusion. The slow erosion of judgment that accompanies advanced age, grief, and dependence.

The diagnosis is not the point. California law does not ask what the doctor called it. It asks whether the person who signed understood what they were signing, and whether someone used that vulnerability to change the outcome.

The person who redirects the estate is sometimes a new spouse. Sometimes a long-estranged child. Sometimes a caretaker who moved into the house a year before the signing. Sometimes a neighbor. Sometimes a professional—an attorney, a financial advisor, an accountant—whose participation made the transaction appear legitimate.

The exploiter's identity varies. The mechanism does not.

One person gains physical control of access to the elder. The family's calls are screened. The locks are changed. Trusted professionals are replaced or worked around. A new estate plan is executed. The family learns what happened after the elder is gone.

What the Book Can Do

I cannot undo what has already happened in any particular case. For many California elder financial abuse and trust contest claims, the limitations window is short—sometimes as little as one hundred and twenty days from formal notice. By the time most families understand what was done, the window is closing or has already closed.

What the book can do is shorten the distance between recognition and action.

It gives a name to what a family is watching while the parent is still alive. It explains what the changed locks mean. The daily phone calls from the newly attentive sibling. The trust restatement executed four days after surgery. The accountant next door, the attorney of thirty-five years, the financial advisor who moved the money.

It can also reach the families who have not yet been harmed but are watching the conditions form. The isolation. The new person in the house. The old friend who is suddenly unavailable by phone. Those families have more time than they know, if they move before the documents are signed.

Someone reading this has already seen a piece of it—a text message that didn't sit right, a Christmas visit that felt wrong, a parent who said on the phone that everything was fine in a voice that was not their parent's voice.

That reader knows something.

This book is for that reader.

The call comes after the funeral. It almost always does.

It does not have to.

One

When It Isn't Alzheimer's

He was sixty-three and drinking a quart of Grey Goose a day. The attorney had known him for thirty-five years.

On an October afternoon in 2024, eight days after Thomas had checked himself out of a Napa rehab program against medical advice, that attorney walked him through a trust amendment. Thomas was visibly shaking. He was texting his wife that there were goblins in the corner.

He had no Alzheimer's diagnosis. He had no dementia workup.

Most people who call me assume that Alzheimer's is the key. No diagnosis, no case.

That is not how the law works.

THE DIAGNOSIS ISN'T THE POINT

California law does not ask what the doctor called it. It asks whether the person who signed understood what they were signing—and whether someone used that vulnerability to change the outcome.

Alzheimer's is the most common path to that vulnerability. It is not the only one.

I have seen it in cases involving Alzheimer's, a silent stroke no one knew had happened, and a man who drank a quart of Grey Goose a day. The diagnosis changes. The mechanism does not.

THE MAN WHO DRANK

Thomas was sixty-three years old. He had been drinking heavily for most of his adult life—a quart of Grey Goose a day by the end.

In the fall of 2024, Thomas's deterioration accelerated. He experienced episodes of transient global amnesia. He reported hallucinations to his doctors. "The room won't stop," he texted his wife. "Something's in the corner." In October, he entered a residential detox program in Napa. He left the next morning against medical advice.

On October 18, 2024—eight days after he had checked himself out of rehab—Thomas had a supervised visit with his eight-year-old son. The supervising physician documented that he arrived by rideshare because he could not drive. He was visibly shaking. He reported that he was seeing goblins and ghosts. He texted his wife during the visit: he was on drugs, he couldn't drive.

That same afternoon, his estate planning attorney walked

him through a trust amendment redirecting assets away from his wife and son.

The attorney had been Thomas's estate planner for both the original trust and this amendment. Thirty-five years of experience. He knew about the rehab admission. He observed Thomas's condition at the signing. He did not document capacity. He did not recommend an independent review.

Thomas was texting his wife from the signing.

I'm on drugs. I can't drive.

There are goblins in the corner.

These signings are described, in depositions, as routine. The attorney arrived at the office. The client signed the papers. Nothing was noted because nothing was noticed. Attorneys who describe the signing this way have usually been practicing long enough that they have forgotten what noticing is supposed to feel like.

Thomas died by suicide in a Sierra cabin in July 2025. His blood alcohol was three times the legal limit.

The Woman Who Was Healing

Margaret was eighty-four years old, recovering from hip replacement surgery. She lived alone in San Mateo County. Her husband Frank had died eight years earlier.

Margaret had maintained the same estate plan for fourteen years—forty percent to her stepson Robert, sixty percent to her stepdaughter Diane. Diane had been there when Margaret went through chemotherapy in the 1990s. Margaret had danced at Robert's wedding and cried with happiness. That April, she stood on the bema at his granddaughter's bat mitzvah, passed the Torah down, and was photographed smiling.

Four days before Margaret's trust was restated—on

September 13, 2024—Diane sent a text message to her brother describing their mother's condition after surgery. "She is doing laundry, going through paperwork, literally on speed. I keep telling her to lay down and she won't. She is going to hurt herself and probably shouldn't have had this surgery."

Four days later, Diane drove Margaret to the attorney's office. The trust was restated. Robert's forty percent share—maintained unchanged for fourteen years through Frank's death, through Margaret's cancer, through everything—was eliminated. The document stated he was "knowingly and intentionally excluded."

Margaret died the following year. Her doctors later identified what the family had been watching: rapidly progressive vascular dementia, the result of a silent stroke she had likely suffered without anyone knowing.

She left a voicemail for Robert's wife in June 2025.

"This isn't a good time right now. I'm a little confused. Di will be here on the 7th through the 12th. Maybe if you call during that time she can get things straightened out."

She died before anything was straightened out.

The letter she wrote to Robert on July 4, 2025, was never mailed. He found out about it on September 11. Her handwriting in it was severely degraded.

Diane's text message is the case. She wrote it herself.

The Diagnosis and the Mechanism

The diagnosis is different. The pattern is the same.

In Thomas's case, the amendment was executed in the days between a failed rehab stay and a documented hallucination episode. In Margaret's case, four days after surgery—during a period her stepdaughter had described as "literally on speed."

And in both cases, it began with access. Thomas's attorney was already in place. Diane called Margaret daily when she had previously rarely called at all. She drove her to the attorney. After Margaret's death, she monitored Robert's visit to the house through a caregiver, texting instructions in real time about what he could and could not take.

The person who controls access controls the outcome. The documents follow.

For the Reader Who Recognizes This

My parent didn't have Alzheimer's. Can we still challenge the trust under California law?

Yes. California law does not require a specific diagnosis to establish lack of capacity or undue influence. Probate Code §§ 810 through 813 ask whether the person understood what they were signing—not what the underlying condition was called. California trust contests have succeeded on the basis of vascular dementia from silent stroke, alcohol-related cognitive decline, post-surgical confusion, and Lewy body dementia that was not diagnosed until autopsy. The diagnosis is not the threshold. The vulnerability at the moment of signing is.

My parent's doctor never evaluated their capacity before the signing. Does that defeat the case?

No. Most people who sign documents during periods of cognitive vulnerability never receive a contemporaneous capacity evaluation, and California law does not require one. Post-death capacity is reconstructed from contemporaneous medical records, communications from the relevant period, the observations of percipient witnesses including the drafting attorney, and the opinions of forensic experts applying the Probate Code § 811 criteria. The absence of a capacity evaluation is the ordinary starting condition of a California trust contest, not a barrier to one.

The attorney who drafted the document has been our family lawyer for decades. Does that protect him?

The opposite. A long-tenured family attorney has the deepest possible record of what the client was like before, and therefore the clearest possible knowledge of what the client was like at the signing. California law does not reduce the standard of care because the relationship is old—it sharpens what the attorney knew or should have known. Under Evidence Code §§ 957 and 961, the attorney's file becomes discoverable on the client's death, and the attorney becomes a witness to the signing and, in many cases, a defendant in the suit. The longer the relationship, the stronger the evidence the relationship produces.

More detailed answers appear in the Appendix: Questions and Answers at the end of this book.

Two

When the Stranger Moves In

I have to marry him before it's too late.

Elliot was eighty-seven years old the first time his children heard Lorraine's name. He had met her at the department store where she worked. She was in her fifties. He was a widower. His wife Ruth had died five years earlier, after fifty-seven years of marriage.

After Ruth's death, the family stayed close. His daughter Nora, who lived nearby, cooked his meals, drove him to his doctor's appointments, and visited nearly every day after her own daughter got out of school. His granddaughter called him her heart.

In 2018, Lorraine and her daughter moved into Elliot's house. Nora came by one afternoon and found the locks had been changed.

That Christmas, the family gathered at the house as they always had. Elliot told them he had proposed to Lorraine. She showed them the ring. Then she stood up from the couch and yelled at his daughter: "I have to marry him before it's too late."

When the children asked about her, they learned she had been married five times before. She had eight children. She had been renting a room in a nearby town before she moved in.

Elliot's daughter Claire told Lorraine that Elliot had a lot to offer, and asked what her intentions were. Lorraine ran through the house screaming that Elliot's children were evil.

Two months later, Elliot called Claire at work. He told her Lorraine wanted to get married and that she kept nagging him about it. He was adamant: he did not want to get married again.

On March 19, 2020, the governor issued a stay-at-home order.

On April 25, 2020—Lorraine's birthday—Elliot married her. He was eighty-nine years old. His children did not learn about the marriage for approximately a year.

What the Pandemic Made Possible

COVID did not cause what happened to Elliot. But it provided the conditions.

Before Lorraine, Elliot's children spoke with him by phone or text every week. They drove to the house regularly. His son drove up from Los Angeles. Claire came from the Central Valley. Nora and her daughter visited after school and on weekends. The grandchildren stayed at the house when they were in town. Elliot was always available.

After Lorraine moved in, and after the stay-at-home orders, that access ended. Lorraine told Nora that visitors were not allowed at the house. When Nora and her daughter came to see Elliot, Lorraine would open the front door slightly but would not let them inside.

The family noticed that Elliot would only call them when Lorraine was not at the house. When Lorraine was present, he did not answer the phone.

By 2020, his children had noticed signs of memory loss.

The isolation was not medical. It was strategic. And it lasted.

The Day Everything Was Signed

On a single day in August 2022—a few days after Elliot's ninety-second birthday—the following documents were executed: a new trust, a new will, a durable power of attorney, a declaration of trust, a certification of trust, an assignment of personal property, and a grant deed transferring the house into the new trust.

All on the same day.

The trust named Lorraine as sole beneficiary. She was named successor trustee. She received the house. She received the personal property. She received the residue of the estate. Elliot's four children—the people he had raised with Ruth over fifty-seven years of marriage—received nothing.

The trust identified Elliot's living children by name.

Every name was misspelled.

His daughter's name was wrong. Another daughter's name was wrong. A third child's married name was wrong. The document that disinherited his children could not spell their names.

Four months later, on Christmas Day 2022, Elliot told his son that his estate was going to be split evenly among his four children when he died.

The trust had already been signed.

THE CREDIT CARDS

Elliot was not a credit card user. He paid for things with cash, checks, or cashier's checks. His credit report confirmed what his family already knew: by October 2019, every one of his credit cards carried a zero balance.

By April 2021, twelve of those cards carried a combined balance of nearly seventy-four thousand dollars.

The charges began after Lorraine moved in.

Lorraine's daughter stole a check from Elliot and wrote herself five thousand dollars. When Elliot discovered it, the daughter was asked to leave.

Lorraine bragged to Elliot's daughter about a nine-thousand-dollar massage chair she had recently purchased.

THE HOSPITAL AND THE PHONE

In the months before his death, Elliot was hospitalized multiple times for urinary tract infections and dehydration. His children were not notified by Lorraine. They learned about the hospitalizations from neighbors who had seen the ambulances arrive at the house.

When Elliot was in the hospital, his children could reach him by phone. They noticed his mood was better. He was accessible. He talked to them the way he always had.

When Lorraine discovered that Elliot was communicating with his family from the hospital, she removed his cellphone from the room. A code was required to call his hospital room directly. Lorraine told the family that Elliot did not want visitors.

One day, a text was sent from Elliot's phone to his daughter: "Don't call me."

She never spoke to her father again.

The family believes Lorraine sent the text.

The Last Days

Elliot was admitted to the hospital for the final time in October 2023. He was discharged to hospice two days later.

The day before he died, Nora saw Lorraine at a local farmer's market. During their conversation, Nora learned that Elliot was at home. Alone. Without Lorraine or a hospice nurse.

A ninety-three-year-old man on hospice, dying, by himself.

Elliot died the next morning.

Nora and her best friend went to the house that afternoon. Lorraine told Nora she couldn't stand the way Elliot was breathing and knew he was transitioning, so she had gone into the next room to sleep. Then Lorraine described the movements Elliot made as he died. She used her arms and hands to demonstrate them.

Nora and her friend were so disturbed they left the room.

Lorraine's daughter moved into the house shortly after the funeral.

Elliot's daughter Claire had filed a report of suspected elder abuse five months before her father died. The report did not stop what was already in motion.

Since Elliot's death, Lorraine has not allowed his children to return to the house to retrieve Ruth's ashes or the family's heirlooms.

Ruth died in 2012. She and Elliot had been married for fifty-seven years. Her ashes were in the house where they had raised their children.

The house that now belongs to Lorraine.

The stranger is one face of the pattern. There is another.

PATRICK AND COLLEEN

Patrick and Colleen O'Dea had been married for decades. They lived in a house in Santa Barbara they had owned since the 1970s. They had three children: Maureen, Brendan, and Siobhan. The family trust, executed in 2005, divided the estate equally among them.

Patrick had a long history of cognitive vulnerability. He had suffered a traumatic brain injury. He had been scammed out of fifty-five thousand dollars by men overseas who manipulated him into wiring them money. After quadruple bypass surgery, he experienced confusion and hallucinations. During recovery, his daughter Siobhan was the only person he was able to recognize.

In 2010, Siobhan moved back in with her parents to help with daily care. She planned to stay six months. She stayed for years. In 2011, her sister Maureen and Maureen's husband moved in. Siobhan moved out.

Within weeks, the locks on the house were changed. Siobhan had held a key to her parents' home for her entire life. She asked Maureen for a new one. Maureen refused.

Patrick and Colleen told Brendan and Siobhan that they loved them and missed them. But they also said they were unable to stand up for themselves to visit or speak with them.

By 2016, Patrick and Colleen had stopped driving. Eventually they stopped returning Siobhan's calls altogether.

On May 13, 2022, Patrick and Colleen executed a restatement of their trust. Patrick was eighty-seven. Colleen was eighty-eight. The restatement eliminated the equal three-way split that had governed since 2005. In its place: fifty percent to

Maureen, fifty percent to Maureen's son. Brendan and Siobhan received nothing.

Patrick and Colleen moved into a skilled nursing facility in November 2023. Colleen died on May 2, 2024. Patrick died twenty days later.

Maureen served the trustee notice the following month.

The Stranger and the Daughter

Elliot's case is the stranger who arrives through a chance encounter and never leaves. The O'Deas' case is the child who was already in the house. The entry points are different. The mechanism is the same.

In both cases, one person gained physical control of the home. In both cases, the locks were changed. In both cases, the other children's access to the parent was systematically reduced and eventually eliminated. In both cases, the parent told family members that the estate plan had not changed—while the documents had already been signed.

And in both cases, the documents were executed during a period when the elder was cognitively compromised, physically dependent, and isolated from the family members who might have intervened.

The law does not distinguish between a stranger and a daughter. It asks the same questions of both: Was the elder vulnerable? Did the person who benefited have authority and control? What tactics were used? And is the result equitable?

In Elliot's case, the answer is written in the trust document itself—in every misspelled name of every child it disinherited.

She said it herself, from the couch, at Christmas, in front of his children.

I have to marry him before it's too late.

For the Reader Who Recognizes This

A new person has moved in with my parent and I'm being kept away. What does California law say about isolation?

California Welfare and Institutions Code § 15610.70 lists isolation as one of the four factors courts weigh in determining undue influence. Isolation includes changed locks, screened calls, restricted visits, intercepted mail, and the systematic control of who sees the elder and when. Under California law, isolation is not itself a cause of action—it is evidence of undue influence. It becomes central later, when a court is asked whether the document signed during the period of control reflects the elder's free will or someone else's.

My parent is still alive. What can I do right now, before documents are signed?

More than you can do after the fact. If your parent still has capacity, she can revoke the existing estate plan, change the locks back, name a new power of attorney, and execute a new trust that reflects what she actually intends. If capacity is uncertain, California offers three intervening tools: a petition for limited conservatorship under Probate Code § 1800 and following; a petition to revoke an improperly executed power of attorney; and, in cases of documented abuse, an Elder or Dependent Adult Abuse Restraining Order under Welfare and Institutions Code § 15657.03. The legal options available to a living parent do not exist after death. This is the moment to use them.

The person controlling access is my sibling, not a stranger. Does California law treat this differently?

The four undue influence factors under California Welfare and Institutions Code § 15610.70—vulnerability, apparent authority, tactics used, and equity of result—apply identically whether the influencer is a stranger, a caregiver, a new spouse, or a sibling. What changes is one evidentiary mechanism: the Probate Code § 21380 presumption that invalidates transfers to drafters and paid care custodians does not apply to close blood relatives, under the § 21382 exception. A sibling can still be the influencer. The case is built through the general § 15610.70 factors and the Probate Code § 811 capacity framework, rather than through § 21380's burden shift.

More detailed answers appear in the Appendix: Questions and Answers at the end of this book.

Three

The People Who Made It Possible

The attorney prepared the documents. The accountant witnessed the signing. None of them picked up the phone.

Richard was eighty-nine years old and dying. He had been in hospice for a week. His stepdaughter Denise had been his primary caretaker for two years—controlling his schedule, managing his medications, deciding who could visit and when.

Twelve days before Richard died, an attorney arrived at the house with a restated trust. The document redirected a three-to-five-million-dollar estate entirely to Denise. Richard's biological children—the people he had raised, the people who bore his name—were eliminated.

The attorney did not come alone. Richard's neighbor, an accountant named Gerald, was there to facilitate the signing. Gerald had known Richard for years. He had watched the cognitive decline. He understood what a restated trust would do to the family.

Gerald was not a bystander. He was the person who made the document operational—the professional whose presence gave the signing an appearance of legitimacy it did not deserve. When the family eventually obtained the records, Gerald's role was documented throughout: communications with the attorney, coordination with Denise, involvement at every stage of the transaction.

California law anticipated Richard's case. A donative transfer to the drafter of the document, or to a caretaker who cared for the elder in the months before it was signed, is presumptively invalid. The family does not have to prove undue influence at the signing. The person who benefited has to prove there was none. Denise was the caretaker. The attorney was the drafter. The presumption runs against both of them.

Richard died in Los Angeles. His children learned what had happened weeks later.

The accountant never called them either.

The Pattern No One Expects

When families call after discovering that a parent's estate was redirected, their anger is focused on the person who benefited. The stepmother. The caretaker. The sibling who was in the room when the documents were signed.

That anger is understandable. It is also incomplete.

In case after case, the exploitation could not have happened without professional help. An attorney who drafted documents for a client whose capacity was visibly compromised. A financial advisor who moved assets at the direction of someone who was not the account holder. An accountant who facilitated a transaction he knew would strip a dying man's children of their inheritance.

These are not peripheral figures. They are the infrastructure of the scheme.

Without the attorney, there is no document. Without the financial advisor, the money does not move. Without the accountant or the notary or the witness who lends professional credibility to an illegitimate signing, the exploitation fails at the point of execution.

An elder financial abuse claim reaches every one of them. Not only the person who ended up with the money—everyone involved in the wrongful taking. The attorney who drafted. The accountant who witnessed. The financial advisor who moved the account. Each is a defendant.

The Attorney Is a Witness

Consider again the man in Chapter One. Sixty-three years old. Grey Goose by the quart. Goblins in the kitchen. Eight days out of a Napa detox program he had checked himself out of against medical advice.

His attorney had known him for thirty-five years. He had drafted the original trust. He knew the wife and son. He knew about the drinking and the rehab and the hallucinations because the man's wife had told him, in the weeks before the signing, that none of it had stopped.

On October 18, 2024, the attorney walked him through a trust amendment that redirected assets away from the wife and son. The client had arrived by rideshare because he could not drive. He was shaking. He was texting his wife during the meeting that he was seeing goblins, that he was on drugs, that he could not drive.

The attorney documented none of it. He did not note the

client's condition. He did not recommend an independent capacity evaluation.

What the attorney did was notarize the document and go home.

Nine months later, the client was dead.

An attorney who drafts a trust amendment for a client whose capacity is in question does not become a neutral professional performing a technical function. He becomes an eyewitness. The law has a term for this—*percipient witness*—and the term determines what happens to him when the trust is contested.

He has no privilege to hide behind for what he observed. The attorney-client privilege protects communications. It does not protect his own perceptions of whether the client understood what he was signing. He saw the shaking. He observed whether the client could track the conversation. He made a judgment call about whether to proceed. That judgment call is testimony.

The privilege does not fully survive the client. In a dispute over what the client actually wanted, the lawyer's file is available to the parties. The privilege exists to protect the client; the dispute is about what he intended. Once he is gone, the file is often the clearest record of his mental state at the moment the document was signed.

The file comes out in a deposition. The pattern of questions is the same, because the patterns in the files are the same.

How long was the meeting. Who scheduled it. Who paid the retainer. Who was in the parking lot. Who walked in with the client. Where did they sit. Did the client open the conversation or did the person next to him. What questions did the client ask. What questions did you ask. What did you notice about how he answered. Did you time-stamp the signing. Did you make notes.

What the file shows is rarely a confession. It is the shape of the meeting. How long it lasted. Who else was in the room. Whether the client asked questions that made sense. Whether the instructions came from the client or from the person sitting next to him. The file usually tells the story. The deposition confirms it.

The second thing that happens to the drafting attorney is disqualification. He is a material witness to the signing he is being asked to defend. He cannot both testify and advocate. He also possesses confidential information from the drafting—the family, the assets, the prior intentions—that makes representing one side against the other untenable.

That is a motion, filed early, that removes the person most invested in defending the signing from the case.

The drafting attorney's conduct in these cases falls along a spectrum. At one end is the attorney who failed to recognize what should have been obvious—who conducted a thirty-minute meeting with a client in cognitive decline and saw nothing wrong. At the other end is the attorney who knew exactly what was happening and drafted the documents anyway—because the person paying the bill was not the person signing the trust.

The legal consequence does not depend heavily on which end of the spectrum the attorney sits at. The file is the file. The deposition is the deposition. The attorney who did not want to see is cross-examined on what was in front of him. The attorney who saw and proceeded is cross-examined on why.

The attorney who walked the sixty-three-year-old man through the amendment that day still practices.

When the Trust Pays for Its Own Destruction

There is a third category of enabler that most families never anticipate.

Nathan was permanently incapacitated—a young man who had never been able to manage his own affairs. Years earlier, a personal injury settlement had placed approximately six million dollars into an irrevocable trust for his lifetime care. The trust named him as the sole primary beneficiary. His family members were named as co-trustees.

For thirteen years, Nathan received no accounting. No one told him—or anyone acting on his behalf—where the money had gone. Trust funds were used to purchase real property titled in family members' names. Trust funds were used for personal expenses that had nothing to do with Nathan's care. The life care plan that justified the original settlement was ignored.

When the misconduct was finally discovered and litigation was filed, the family did what families in these situations always do: they hired a defense attorney. And they paid that attorney with trust funds.

The money that was supposed to care for Nathan for the rest of his life was now being used to defend the people who had taken it.

This is the point most families miss.

When trustees who are accused of misappropriating trust assets use those same assets to pay their defense lawyers, every dollar spent is an additional act of financial abuse. The exploitation does not stop when the petition is filed. It accelerates.

California law is clear on this. A trustee's right to be reimbursed from trust assets for legal expenses is strictly limited to expenses properly incurred in the administration of the trust.

Where the trustee's conduct constitutes a breach of fiduciary duty, the right to indemnification is forfeited. You cannot use the trust's money to defend yourself against the trust's beneficiary for stealing the trust's money. The logic is circular. The law does not permit it.

The defense attorney who accepts those fees is not an innocent third party. Trust property can be recovered from any person who holds it—not only from fiduciaries. The statute reaches any third-party recipient. An attorney who receives trust funds knowing those funds are claimed trust property stands in the same legal posture as a family member who received a fraudulent transfer. The mechanism of diversion—legal fees rather than real property—does not alter the analysis. Once formal notice has been given that the fees are unauthorized, continued acceptance is a choice, and the choice carries personal liability for the lawyer.

Look at Who Made It Possible

If you are reading this chapter because your parent's estate was redirected, you are focused on the person who benefited. That is natural.

Look at who made it possible.

Who drafted the trust amendment. Who managed the financial accounts. Who witnessed the signing. And now—if litigation has been filed or is being considered—who is paying the defense lawyers. If the answer is the trust or the estate, then the exploitation is ongoing.

Every legal fee paid from trust assets to defend the people who took those assets is an additional breach, an additional act of financial abuse, and an additional basis for recovery.

The enablers are not footnotes to the case. They may be the strongest claims you have.

Gerald's name is in every document. He is still living next door.

For the Reader Who Recognizes This

Can the attorney who drafted the trust be sued in California?

Yes. Under California Welfare and Institutions Code § 15657.7, a drafting attorney whose participation made a wrongful transaction possible can be named as a defendant in a financial elder abuse action. Liability attaches where the attorney knew or reasonably should have known that the client lacked capacity or was being subjected to undue influence, and drafted the document anyway. The attorney who wrote the instrument is not a peripheral figure in California trust litigation. In many cases, the strongest claim the family has runs through him.

The trust is paying the defense lawyers. Is that allowed?

Not where the trustee's own conduct is what's being challenged. Under California Probate Code § 15684, a trustee may be reimbursed from the trust only for expenses properly incurred in the administration of the trust. A trustee defending allegations of breaching fiduciary duty cannot fund that defense with the assets the beneficiaries are seeking to recover. The California decisions in *Pizarro v. Reynoso* and *Kasperbauer v. Fairfield* develop the point. Trust funds already paid out can be recovered through a Probate Code § 850 petition, and a defense attorney formally notified that the fees are unauthorized has actual knowledge under the law. Every legal fee paid from the trust becomes an additional basis for recovery.

The person who took the estate has no money left. Is the case worth bringing?

Often yes, because California financial elder abuse law reaches beyond the person who received the money. Under Welfare and Institutions Code § 15657.7, every professional whose participation made the wrongful transaction possible can be named as a defendant—the drafting attorney, the care custodian who provided services in the 90 days before signing, the notary who completed a signing she should have questioned, the financial advisor who moved money at someone else's direction, the accountant who facilitated the transfer. These are not peripheral claims. They are often the claims that produce recovery, because professionals carry insurance and firms carry assets. The estate may be empty. The case is rarely empty with it.

More detailed answers appear in the Appendix: Questions and Answers at the end of this book.

Four

The Envelope That Looked Like Nothing

The letter arrived on a Tuesday. She opened it. She read it once. She put it in the stack with the condolence cards.

Karen was fifty-six. Her father had died five weeks earlier, in the house he had built in the 1970s outside Roseville. Her stepmother had been in the house for the last nine years of his life. Karen had flown out for the funeral. She had flown home to Oregon the following Monday. Her father had told her for years that his estate would provide for her.

The letter arrived on a Tuesday. It was one page. The letterhead said it was from a law firm she had never heard of. It identified a trust by name, named the trustee—her stepmother—and stated that a copy of the trust instrument was available on request. It referred to a Probate Code section.

Karen read the letter once. She understood the words. She did not understand what the letter was.

She put it in a plastic file where she kept sympathy cards, her father's death certificate, the hospital billing that was still arriving from the last weeks, and a folder labeled Dad—miscellaneous that she intended to go through when she had the energy. It was March. She was back at work. Her husband was getting ready for a trial. Her son was finishing his junior year of high school.

She thought about the letter twice in the weeks that followed. Both times she thought she should probably ask someone what it meant. Both times she did not.

In late July, her brother called. He had received the same letter. He had called a lawyer that afternoon.

The lawyer had told him the letter was a statutory notice. It had been served on March 3. Under California law, a beneficiary or heir had one hundred and twenty days from the date of service to contest the trust. One hundred and twenty days had been June 30.

It was July 23.

The grounds Karen and her brother would have raised—that their father lacked capacity when the trust was restated in his final year, that their stepmother had exerted undue influence, that the document triggered a presumption of invalidity because the stepmother had been his caregiver—were largely gone. Not in every form. Not for every claim. But the trust contest itself had closed on June 30, and the hardest-working statutory presumptions had closed with it.

Karen pulled the letter out of the plastic file. It was the same letter she had opened in March. It had not changed.

What the Notice Does

The letter was a statutory notice. Under California law, the trustee of a trust that has become irrevocable at death must serve it within sixty days. Once served, the recipient has one hundred and twenty days to file a contest. Capacity. Undue influence. Fraud. The presumptions that apply to drafters and caregivers. After one hundred and twenty days, those grounds are largely gone.

One hundred and twenty days is not a long time in the life of a grieving family. A daughter in another state, a son finishing a trial, a brother negotiating with a landlord—these are the conditions in which the clock runs. The envelope looks like nothing because the envelope has been designed, across decades of estate practice, to look like nothing. One page. Formal language. A reference to a statute that means nothing to the person reading it. It is easy to miss. It is meant to be easy to miss.

The trustee who took the estate is also, by operation of law, the person who starts the clock on the family's ability to challenge her. There is no irony in the design. The statute was written to give families notice. In cases where the trustee is adverse to the family—which is every case in this book—the notice is technically served and practically invisible.

Karen's notice was valid. The clock had run.

What Karen Still Had

This is the part of the chapter a reader who has received a letter like Karen's needs.

The trust contest was closed. It was not the only claim.

Financial elder abuse claims run four years from discovery,

not from death. Karen had not known, in March, that her father's capacity had been questionable in the months before the restatement. She had not known that his caregiver had been driving him to the attorney. She had not known that the attorney's file, when it was eventually obtained, would show a pattern of meetings that matched the deterioration in her father's medical records. By the time she learned those things, she had a claim under the elder abuse statute, and the four-year clock on that claim had not yet begun to run.

Post-window abuse claims are strongest where they reach defendants the trust contest would not have reached—the drafting attorney, the caregiver, the financial advisor whose participation made the transaction possible. The statute reaches the stepmother. It also reaches each of those enablers, where the facts support it. Attorney's fees are mandatory on recovery. Damages are doubled on a finding of bad faith.

Karen had something else, which is the piece most families miss. California law allows property wrongfully transferred to be recovered from whoever is holding it. The house her father had built in the 1970s, if it had been transferred by the restated trust and remained in the stepmother's hands, was reachable. Not by the contest the clock had closed. By the recovery petition that runs on a different clock and a different theory.

The daughter who walks into a lawyer's office six weeks after the 120-day window has closed is often told the case is over. The daughter whose lawyer knows this area of law well is told the case is different than she thought.

THE NEIGHBOR

Ellen was forty-nine. Her father had died the previous March in San Jose, a year before she walked into my office. He had lived alone in the Willow Glen house since her mother's death in 2019. A caregiver named Marisol had been in the house five days a week for the last eighteen months of his life. Ellen lived in Sacramento. She drove down on weekends when she could. Her brother was in Seattle and came out less often.

The statutory notice had arrived four weeks after the death. Ellen had read it. She had called the number on the letterhead and asked for a copy of the trust. The trust had arrived in the mail a week later. It was not the trust Ellen's father had shown her in 2017. A restatement executed in September of the last year of his life had redirected the bulk of the estate to Marisol and to Marisol's adult son, whom Ellen had met once. Ellen and her brother each received a specific bequest of forty thousand dollars.

Ellen had been angry. She had been tired. She had called her brother. They had talked about whether to contest. They had not known what contesting meant in any specific sense. The bequests were not nothing. Ellen had a daughter starting college. Her brother's wife was between jobs. They had agreed, on the phone in late May, that they would take the forty thousand and not fight.

The 120-day window closed at the end of July.

In March of the following year—a year after the death—Ellen drove down to San Jose for the one-year memorial her brother had organized at the Willow Glen house. The house had been sold by Marisol in November. The memorial was at a restaurant the father had liked. About thirty people came. One of them was a neighbor named Jim who had lived across the street from the father for twenty-two years.

Jim told Ellen, standing near the bar with a glass of wine, that he had watched Marisol drive her father to the same office in Campbell at least six times in the fall before he died. He had noticed because the father had stopped driving the previous summer and the appointments were on Tuesday mornings, when Jim was home, and he had been curious whether the father was seeing a new doctor. He had asked Marisol once, at the mailbox, what kind of appointments they were. She had told him they were for the father's tax attorney.

The father had used the same tax attorney for thirty years. The attorney's office was in downtown San Jose, not Campbell.

Ellen asked Jim how certain he was. Jim said he was certain. He had seen the car leave on Tuesday mornings and return on Tuesday afternoons for most of the fall. He had mentioned it to his wife at the time. His wife remembered the conversations.

Ellen called me on a Thursday in April.

She told me the case was closed. The 120-day window had run in July. She was calling, she said, because she wanted to understand what had been done to her father even if nothing could be done about it. She did not ask me, in that first call, whether there was a claim.

I asked her the questions I ask. What the neighbor had seen. When he had seen it. Whether his wife would confirm the conversations at the time. Whether the father's medical records for that fall were obtainable. Whether the restated trust named the attorney who had drafted the original, or a different attorney. Whether Marisol was still living in the area. Whether the house had sold to an arm's-length buyer.

The answers were the answers that make a case. The neighbor was local and articulate and his wife remembered the conversations. The medical records were at Kaiser and would be produced on a release. The restated trust named an attorney in Campbell whom I had not heard of but whose office matched the address the neighbor had described. Marisol had moved to

Gilroy. The house had sold at market to a buyer with no apparent connection.

The trust contest had closed in July. That claim was gone.

The abuse claim had not closed. Ellen's discovery—the neighbor at the memorial—was less than a month old when she called me. The four-year clock had just begun to run. The claim reached Marisol. It reached the Campbell attorney. It reached Marisol's son if the transfers to him rose to the level the statute requires. And because Marisol was a caregiver in the months before the signing, the statutory presumption against caregivers applied to the transfers to her—an evidentiary tool that survives the closing of the contest window and shifts the burden to the recipient to prove the transfer was not the product of undue influence.

The evidence was fresh. The witnesses were alive. The records existed.

Ellen asked me whether the case was worth pursuing. I told her what I tell families in this posture. The abuse claim does not recover the house—the arm's-length buyer is protected—but it reaches the proceeds of the sale, which Marisol had received five months earlier. It reaches the attorney, whose liability depends on what the file shows and what his practice records support. And it reaches the son, depending on what the records show about what he received and when.

I told her the case could be filed in thirty days. I told her the first step was a preservation letter to the attorney and to Marisol and to the financial institutions that had held the father's accounts. I told her the second step was the medical records. I told her the third step was a conversation with the neighbor, recorded with his consent, to lock in what he had told her at the memorial before memory faded.

Ellen said she had assumed she was too late.

I told her what she already, by that point in the conversation, understood.

She was early.

The Envelope and the Memorial

Karen received a letter in the mail. Ellen heard something at a memorial. One missed a clock she did not know was running. One learned about a clock she did not know existed.

Between them is the entire legal terrain on which a family either recovers or does not. The trust contest closes fast and quietly. The abuse claim runs longer and reaches further. A third claim, narrower than both, runs on its own clock—the one that applies when a parent promised a child that something would come on death, and the child relied on the promise, and the document does something else. The next chapter sorts all three.

Karen learned about the clocks in July. By the time she understood which one had governed her, the one she needed had already closed. By the time she understood which one had not, she was sitting across from a lawyer in Sacramento with a file her stepmother did not yet know existed.

Ellen learned about the clocks in April. By the time she understood which one governed her, she had four years and a case.

The envelope arrived in the mail. The neighbor was at the bar.

For the Reader Who Recognizes This

I received a notice months ago and didn't understand what it was. Have I missed the window?

Possibly. Possibly not. The 120-day trust contest window under California Probate Code § 16061.7 closes 120 days after proper service of a compliant notice. Two things commonly extend the window. First, if the notice did not include the trust and you requested one, the window runs until the later of 120 days or 60 days from the date the trust was delivered. Second, a notice that fails to meet the statutory content requirements—missing the warning language, wrong beneficiary list, wrong address—does not start the clock at all. Before concluding the window has closed, have a California attorney review the actual notice.

What do I do this week if the 120-day clock has already run?

Two things. First, preserve everything—the notice, the trust, the will, medical records, texts, emails, photographs, any documents from the period before and after the signing. The four-year financial elder abuse clock under California Welfare and Institutions Code § 15657.7 is often still open even after the 120-day window closes, and the evidence that supports it decays fast. Second, schedule a consultation with a California trust litigation attorney. The 120-day clock is only one of three. The elder abuse clock reaches further, lasts longer, and often carries the strongest claims against drafting attorneys, caregivers, and financial advisors.

My sibling said we should just accept what we were given and not fight. Is that the right call?

It depends on what you were given, what the facts actually support, and what evidence is available. Many families accept early distributions in the first weeks after a death because the distributions are a known quantity and litigation is not. That calculation is rational when the underlying case is weak. It is often wrong when the case is strong—because the distribution you were offered is typically a small fraction of what proper accounting and recovery would yield. Before accepting and waiving further claims, have a California attorney review the facts. One consultation usually answers the question.

More detailed answers appear in the Appendix: Questions and Answers at the end of this book.

Five

The First Thirty Days

She has the trust in her hand. She has read it twice. The first time it didn't make sense. The second time it made too much sense.

The estate went to her brother. To her father's second wife. To a caretaker whose name she has only heard in the last six months. To the stepdaughter who moved into the house during COVID and never moved out.

The funeral was ten days ago.

She doesn't know that a clock is running.

She doesn't know that another clock is running faster.

This chapter is for her. It is also for anyone who has just recognized, from the preceding pages, that the pattern in a parent's estate is the pattern in this book. The recognition itself is the start of the thirty days. What she does between now and the end of them will shape what is possible after.

THE CLOCKS

There are three of them, and most families do not know about any.

The first runs one hundred and twenty days from the service of the statutory notice. Probate Code § 16061.7. The trust contest. Capacity. Undue influence. Fraud. The § 21380 presumption that applies to drafters and caregivers. After one hundred and twenty days, those grounds are largely gone.

Two practical points about the 120-day clock. First, if the notice does not include a copy of the trust, the recipient can request one. The trustee must provide it. The contest window then runs until the later of one hundred and twenty days from the notice or sixty days from the date the trust is delivered. Second, a defective notice—wrong address, wrong beneficiary list, missing the statutorily mandated warning language—does not start the clock at all. Families who assume the clock has run are sometimes wrong about whether it ever started.

A reader whose notice arrived on December 1 has until approximately April 1 to file. A reader whose notice arrived in an envelope she assumed was a condolence card, and who did not open it until March, has until April 1 regardless.

The hundred and twenty days is the first clock. Two more.

The second clock is longer and more forgiving. Financial elder abuse claims run four years. Welfare and Institutions Code § 15657.7. The four years runs from discovery, not from the signing. The clock is delayed-discovery tolled.

What discovery means in practice matters. A daughter who learns in 2026 that her father signed a trust amendment in 2021 —during a period she later realizes he was already symptomatic —does not have a 2025 problem. She has a 2030 problem. Concealment tolls the clock. Isolation tolls the clock. The discovery event is often the death itself, when the family first reads the trust.

That is the statute that reaches the drafters, the caregivers, the financial advisors, the accountants. It is the statute under which attorney's fees are mandatory on recovery and damages are doubled on a finding of bad faith. For most readers of this chapter, it is the primary claim.

The third clock is narrow. One year from death. It applies to a specific kind of claim: the one that arises from a promise. A father tells his daughter, for years, that the farm will come to her if she stays. She stays. The trust says otherwise. Code of Civil Procedure § 366.3 gives her one year.

Three clocks. Read together, they produce a counterintuitive truth.

You may have less time than you think on the trust contest. You have more time than you think on the abuse claim. Both require moving now, and neither is a reason to wait.

The reason both require moving now is not only the law. It is the money, and it is the evidence.

The money does not wait. Trust assets get spent. Real property gets sold. Accounts get transferred to institutions the family cannot reach. Beneficiaries move out of state, and some move further than that. A family that waits two years to file often discovers that the estate they are fighting over no longer exists in a form that can be recovered.

Neither does the evidence. Emails are deleted. Financial institutions purge records. Witnesses move, retire, die. Memories become unreliable.

A four-year clock is the outer wall. It is not the reason to wait.

A brief word to the reader who believes her clock has already run. It often has not. The defective-notice point above is real, and so is delayed discovery on the abuse claim. Families who assume they are too late are sometimes wrong about which clock governs them. A single consultation with a lawyer who has done this work will tell them.

These calculations are made, in the first phone calls, after the family has already assumed the case is closed. It is often not closed. It is often closing.

If you are reading this and you do not know whether you have received formal notice, stop reading. Find the envelope. Look at the postmark.

Before You Call a Lawyer

What a family does in the first days after discovery shapes what any lawyer can do in the months after. Four moves, in priority order.

Preserve.

The evidence in this book—the text Diane sent about her mother's post-surgical state, the voicemail Margaret left before she died, the children's names misspelled in Elliot's trust, the hospital text that said "Don't call me"—is all evidence the families kept. Emails, texts, voicemails, letters, photographs, recordings. Screenshots of text threads with visible dates. Copies of documents. Forward important emails to a dedicated email address so that a subsequent deletion does not eliminate the record. Do not delete anything from the months preceding or following the signing. The thing that looks trivial now may be central at deposition.

Write down what you remember, dated.

Memory decays. Contemporaneous notes do not. The last phone call. The Christmas that felt wrong. The day the locks changed. The day the caregiver moved in. The doctor's waiting-room visit where the parent could not recall the year. Each entry dated to when the event happened, as best the writer can reconstruct, and dated to when the note itself was written. Do not edit older entries. Add to them if new memories surface, but leave the original observation intact.

Do not confront.

The instinct is to call the person who took the estate and demand answers. The instinct is human. The cost is strategic. A phone call in the first week gives the other side a preview of the case, destroys the element of surprise that a well-timed preservation letter provides, and frequently produces recorded statements the family later wishes they had not made. Wait. The conversation that needs to happen will happen, under counsel's direction, with preservation obligations already in place.

Do not sign.

Settlement offers, waivers, receipts, and releases arrive early in some estates. A signature on a document in week two can foreclose a recovery in month three. If anything arrives asking for a signature—from the trustee, from counsel for the estate, from a financial institution—set it aside until a lawyer of the family's choosing reviews it.

These four moves can be made in the first week. They do not require a lawyer. They do require the family to understand that the period before counsel is retained is itself part of the case.

One tool that does require a lawyer is worth naming here, because it moves fastest.

The preservation letter. A lawyer can send one in the first week, often within forty-eight hours of the initial meeting. It goes to the trustee, to the drafting attorney, to financial institutions holding trust assets, and to any other party whose records are likely to matter. It creates a legal duty to retain records—

emails, transaction histories, internal notes, communications with the decedent—and it triggers spoliation consequences if records are subsequently destroyed. The family's first act of legal leverage often happens before a petition is filed.

In the cases that are recovered, preservation begins before the lawyer is hired. In the cases that are not, it begins too late.

THE LAWYER CALL

The first meeting with counsel is not a free conversation about grief. It is an intake. A lawyer who does this work well will run it like one.

The meeting usually runs an hour. Sometimes longer on a complex estate. The lawyer takes notes throughout. Questions will feel intrusive and will cover ground the family has never discussed outside the house. The lawyer is not being rude. The lawyer is building the case.

What to bring.

The § 16061.7 notice, if you have it. The trust and any amendments. The will. The death certificate. Dated notes from the week before. Preserved evidence, organized by date. A list of assets the family knows about and a list of assets it does not. A list of the people who were in the house during the last year of the decedent's life—family, caregivers, neighbors, visitors, professionals.

What the lawyer will ask.

When the person died. When the challenged document was signed. Who was in the room at the signing. Who benefited. What the pattern of the relationship looked like in the last year—who called, who visited, who drove to the doctor, who managed the medications. Whether the reader is a beneficiary under a prior instrument, an heir at law, or both.

Whether the reader remains in the current trust at all, even in reduced form. Whether the § 16061.7 notice has been received, and when. The rough size of the estate and what is known about its composition—real property, accounts, business interests.

What the lawyer should tell you.

Whether the claim is actionable on the facts as described. Which theories are available—undue influence, incapacity, elder financial abuse, trustee breach, § 21380 presumption, fraud. Whether the clock is running and how much time remains. What the first filing is likely to be, and when.

How the case will be funded. California trust and elder abuse matters are typically structured on a contingency, an hourly retainer, or a hybrid that combines both. Contingency shifts the financial risk from the client to the lawyer and is common when recovery prospects are strong and the estate is sufficient to warrant it. Hourly engagements are more common when the issues are complex, when the estate is smaller, or when the client wants more control. A hybrid charges a reduced hourly rate against a smaller contingency. A lawyer who does this work should explain the options in plain terms and recommend the structure best suited to the facts.

Most trust contests and elder abuse cases in California settle. Trial is comparatively rare. Settlement often happens at mediation, after documents have been exchanged and the first depositions taken—typically twelve to thirty months after filing. The recovery in a settled case is almost never the full amount claimed. The recovery in a tried case is occasionally more, occasionally less, and always subject to appeal.

A lawyer who promises a quick result has not read the file. A lawyer who guarantees recovery on the first call should be treated with the skepticism the guarantee warrants. The honest read, offered in the first meeting, is more valuable than the confident one.

The families who recover are not usually the families with the most money. They are the families who move first.

THE TOOLS THAT ARE AVAILABLE

California law gives a family more tools than most families know exist. What follows is not exhaustive. It is a glossary of leverage, grouped by situation.

When the elder is dead.

The trust contest, filed within the § 16061.7 window, challenges the document itself. Grounds: capacity, undue influence, fraud, the § 21380 presumption. The financial elder abuse claim, reaching beneficiaries and enablers both, carries mandatory attorney's fees on recovery and doubled damages on a finding of bad faith. A transfer to the person who drafted the document—or to a caregiver who was there in the months before the signing—is presumptively invalid. The person who benefited has to prove the transfer was not the product of undue influence. The burden shifts. The § 850 petition recovers property wrongfully transferred. It reaches third parties who hold trust assets. Trustee removal and suspension under § 17200 addresses the trustee who is actively harming the estate. Compelled accounting forces disclosure of what the trustee has been doing.

When assets may be dissipated.

The preservation letter, already named, creates the duty to retain records. Lis pendens records a public notice of the pending claim on real property. A bona fide purchaser cannot buy around it. Temporary trustee appointment replaces a sitting trustee during litigation, when the trustee cannot be trusted to preserve the estate. TROs and preliminary injunctions freeze financial accounts where dissipation is imminent. These tools work best when deployed early—before the house is sold, before the account is moved, before the money is spent.

When enablers benefited.

Elder abuse claims reach the drafting attorney, the financial advisor, the accountant, or the caregiver whose participation made the transaction possible. Chapter Four described this framework in detail. Third-party liability for receiving trust property reaches professionals who were compensated from exploited assets. Disqualification motions remove the drafting attorney from defending the document he created—a significant strategic win in many cases.

When the defense is paid from the estate.

A trustee accused of misappropriating trust assets forfeits the right to be indemnified from those assets for his defense. Fee disgorgement motions recover the trust funds already spent on the defense. Personal liability attaches to the defense lawyer who continues to accept trust funds after formal notice that the fees are contested. This was the argument Chapter Four made at length, and it is one of the strongest pieces of leverage a family has once litigation is underway.

These are the tools. Which one applies depends on the case. A lawyer who has done this work will name them in the first meeting and explain which ones fit the family's facts.

The clock is a closing door.

Moving in week two is materially different from moving in month four. The book has shown why, across six chapters: the evidence decays, the witnesses scatter, the assets dissipate, the statutory windows close. The thirty days that follow recognition are not a grace period. They are the case.

The reader at the beginning of this chapter is still holding the document. She has read it twice. She does not yet know which clock governs her. She does not yet know which tools apply.

She looks at the envelope on the table. She picks up the phone.

The letter was never mailed. The call can still be made.

Six

Through the Screen

The phone still rings forty times a week. But the call is different now.

For most of my practice, the exploitation came through the front door. Someone lived in the house. Someone drove the elder to the attorney. The pattern required proximity.

That is no longer the case.

The calls I take now come from families whose parent lost three hundred thousand dollars, eight hundred thousand dollars, one million, two million, three million—to someone who never stood in the house. Who was not in California. Who in many cases was not in the United States.

The door does not have to be in the same state as the person opening it.

TECH SUPPORT

The call comes in on a Friday afternoon. A daughter in the Bay Area. Her father is eighty-one, a retired engineer, widowed four years. He lives alone in the house where he raised her. He has his routines. Morning paper. Walk to the coffee shop. Afternoon with the Wall Street Journal. Crossword before bed.

Two weeks ago a window opened on his computer. A warning. His system had been compromised. His accounts were at risk. A phone number on the screen. Microsoft. Or what looked like Microsoft.

He called the number. The technician was calm and professional. He asked the father to download a small program that would let him see the computer. The father downloaded it. The technician showed him the infection on the screen—moving files, flashing warnings, things the father had never seen before. He explained that the fix required access to the father's bank accounts to confirm they had not been touched.

The father gave him the access. He watched the technician log in. He watched the balances appear on the screen. The technician said the accounts were safe. Then he said he had identified the source of the infection—it had come from a foreign account that had tried to initiate a transfer. To confirm the protection was working, he needed the father to wire a specific amount to a secure holding account. The wire would be refunded within twenty-four hours.

The father wired the money. Then he wired more. Over the course of two weeks he wired three hundred and forty thousand dollars. He believed every wire was going to be refunded.

On the fourteenth day his daughter found the statements.

She called my office. I asked her the questions I ask now. Had the wires gone through traditional bank transfers or through cryptocurrency. Did the father still have remote-access software on his computer. Had the account numbers been provided by the technician or by the father. Had any of the transfers been to domestic accounts.

The answers were the answers I have heard dozens of times. Bank wires, then crypto. The remote-access software was still running when she called. The account numbers came from the technician. The first transfer went to a bank in Hong Kong. The rest went to wallets.

I told her to call her father's bank and have the wires disputed, although the window was closing. I told her to take his computer to a security firm and have the remote-access software removed. I told her to file a report with her local police and with the FBI's Internet Crime Complaint Center. I told her to put a freeze on his credit and change every password.

I did not tell her I could recover the money.

The money was gone.

The Relationship

He was seventy-four. Widowed for eleven years. His wife had been sick for a long time at the end, and the years since had been quiet in a way he had not fully made peace with. He lived in a two-bedroom condominium a son had helped him buy after the house became too much. He played golf on Saturdays with two men he had known since college. He had three grandchildren he saw at Christmas.

He met her on a dating site. That is what he called it, to his daughter, the first time he mentioned her name. A dating site. He said it almost apologetically, as if he should not need such a thing at his age. Her name was Irina. She was forty-eight. She lived in the Czech Republic, she said. She was a widow. She had one daughter.

He wrote to her for four weeks before he sent her any money. In that time he learned about her apartment in Prague, her late husband who had been a civil engineer, her daughter who was studying medicine in Brno. He sent her photographs of his grandchildren. She told him she had wept at the picture of the three of them on a beach.

The first request was for two thousand dollars. Her daughter's tuition had come due and a grant had not been processed in time. He sent it through a wire service. She wrote back the next day. She had received the wire. She could not believe he had done this for her. She had never had a man in her life who was so kind.

Over the next eleven months, he wired her eight hundred and twenty thousand dollars.

The requests came in waves. Her mother was sick and needed surgery. Her daughter's apartment had been burglarized. A tax authority in Prague had put a lien on her accounts and she needed to clear it before she could travel. She had wanted, for months, to come to California to meet him. Every wave had a timeline. Every wire was going to be the last wire before she finally came.

His son found the wire transfer records when he was helping his father with tax preparation in the spring. He recognized, within twenty minutes of looking at the statements, what he was seeing. He called me the same afternoon.

The money was gone. The money had been gone for most of a year. What the son wanted to know was whether there was any way to prevent his father from sending more. Whether the dating site could be made to disclose what it knew about the woman. Whether an investigator could identify her.

On the last question, I told him what I tell families in this position. An investigator can sometimes identify the network the communications passed through. Sometimes a photograph can be traced to its actual source—often a woman in another country whose image was scraped from her social media without her knowledge. Sometimes the bank accounts that received the wires can be linked to other victims, and a pattern can be assembled. None of this typically recovers the money. It sometimes helps with the decision to stop.

He asked about the decision to stop. His father was still writing to her. Still believed she was real. Still believed she was coming to California.

The son was about to tell his father that the woman he loved did not exist. I told him to do it with his father's own doctor present, if he could arrange it. And I told him that in my experience the father would not believe him. Not at first. The relationship was real to the father. The money he had sent, to the father's mind, was a proof of that reality—if the relationship was a lie, then the money had been a decade of his careful saving thrown into a fire, and no one can accept that in one conversation.

The son called me three weeks later. His father had believed him on the fourth attempt. He had stopped writing. He was not speaking much to anyone, including his son.

The money was still gone.

Guaranteed Returns

A husband and wife in their late seventies. Comfortable. Two adult children. Thirty-five years in the same house. A portfolio put together by a financial advisor they had used for decades, generating enough retirement income that they lived comfortably without touching principal.

The husband was approached on a messaging application by a woman who claimed to be a friend of a friend from his college fraternity. She introduced him, over the course of several weeks of casual conversation, to a proprietary cryptocurrency trading platform. She showed him her own account on the platform. Her returns were exceptional. She had been trading for eighteen months. The platform was invitation-only. She would vouch for him.

He put in ten thousand dollars. The platform showed his balance growing. Within two weeks it showed twenty-two thousand. He withdrew two thousand as a test. The withdrawal processed. He put in fifty thousand more.

Over the next six months the husband wired the platform approximately two million dollars. The platform's dashboard showed his balance at eleven million. He planned, when the balance reached fifteen, to withdraw everything and tell his wife what he had been doing. He intended to surprise her with the gain. It would change what his children would inherit. It would change what he and his wife could do with the years they had left.

He tried to make a withdrawal in the sixth month. The platform required a tax clearance fee of three hundred thousand dollars before the withdrawal could process. He did not have three hundred thousand dollars in liquid assets. He told his wife, for the first time, what he had been doing. He told her in order to explain why he needed her to agree to sell a rental property they had owned since the 1980s.

She called their daughter.

The daughter called me.

She was an accomplished professional. A lawyer herself,

though not in my field. She had read carefully before she called. She had assembled the wire records, the screenshots of the platform, the messages between her father and the woman who had introduced him to it. She understood what she was looking at before she said it out loud.

She took me through it chronologically. The first contact. The first wire. The growing balance. The withdrawal that processed. The larger wires. The dashboard showing eleven million dollars. The tax clearance fee. The phone call when her father told her mother. The moment her mother called her, which was the moment the daughter understood that her parents had lost three million dollars of their savings to someone they had never met.

She asked me what could be done.

I told her what I have told the other families. Report it to her local police department. Report it to the FBI's Internet Crime Complaint Center. The platform was a spoof, generated to show whatever balance the operators wanted a given victim to see. The money had not been invested in anything. It had moved, over the six months, through a chain of accounts in jurisdictions that do not cooperate with U.S. recovery efforts, and by the time her father tried to withdraw, the funds had been converted to assets and physical currency that cannot be traced.

I told her that what she was watching was a pattern called pig-butchering. She said she had never heard that phrase. I told her that did not matter.

She asked whether there was any civil remedy. Any attorney who specialized in this. Any investigator who had recovered funds in a case like hers.

There was not. The money was long gone and beyond U.S. jurisdiction.

She asked if there was anything else.

I told her no. File the reports. Protect her father from further solicitation. Make sure the family's remaining accounts were frozen to new wires. Hold on to what was left.

She thanked me. She was composed on the phone.

I thought, when she hung up, of her walking into her parents' living room and sitting down across from her father to tell him what I had just told her.

Three million dollars.

Gone.

These cases do not arrive at my office as trust contests. They come earlier, and they come alone. The family calls because the money is gone, not because a document is in dispute.

But the money that is gone is the money that would have been in the estate. The retirement account that funded the wire to Hong Kong is the retirement account that would have passed to the children. The rental property sold to cover the tax clearance fee is the rental property that would have funded the widow's care. The portfolio that the advisor built over four decades, liquidated wire by wire to a woman in the Czech Republic who did not exist, is the portfolio that would have carried a man into his nineties.

The estate was exploited before the estate document was signed. That is the point of the chapter, and it takes a moment to see. The elder who has wired eight hundred thousand dollars to a woman he has never met is the elder whose judgment has been shown, in the most visible possible way, to be compromised—to himself, to his family, to anyone watching. The scammer is the first person to have read that vulnerability. He is rarely the last.

The caretaker who arrives six months later reads the same signs. The neighbor who starts coming by every afternoon reads them. The child, long estranged, who reappears at a difficult moment reads them. Each of them sees an elder whose family has already fought one losing argument with him and is tired. Each of them sees an estate that is already smaller than it should have been, which makes what remains easier to move. The drafter who rewrites the trust during the next hospitalization is the fourth person, not the first, to have noticed.

The door that opened through the screen is the door that opens the other doors.

The Advisor's File

There is one more reader who was typically watching, and whose job was to see.

In most of the cases that reach my office, somebody else saw the wires before the family did. A registered investment advisor who had managed the accounts for a decade. A broker-dealer whose compliance system flagged the transfers as unusual. A bank relationship manager who recognized the father across the counter and knew he had not wired money overseas in his life.

These professionals had duties the scammer did not have. The scammer owed the elder nothing. The advisor owed the elder everything the law asks of a fiduciary—the duty to know the client, the duty of care, the duty to act in the client's best interest, the duty to escalate when the facts warrant it.

The question I ask in the first call, after the wires and the platform and the woman in Prague, is what the advisor did.

Registered investment advisors in the United States are fiduciaries. They owe their clients a duty of care and a duty of loyalty. In California, elder clients are owed more. The state's financial elder abuse statute reaches conduct that assists in the wrongful taking of an elder's property. An advisor who processes wires the advisor knows, or reasonably should know, are being sent to a fraud is not outside the statute. The advisor is inside it.

Broker-dealers operate under a different framework but arrive at a similar place. FINRA rules authorize a member firm to place a temporary hold on disbursements when the firm reasonably believes financial exploitation is occurring. Separate rules require firms to obtain the name and contact information of a trusted contact person for each senior client's account. Regulation Best Interest governs the broker-dealer's conduct standard with retail clients. None of these rules makes the firm the elder's guardian. All of them make it impossible, on the current state of the regulations, for a firm to say it had no duty to notice.

The federal Senior Safe Act provides immunity to financial institutions that report suspected exploitation in good faith. The immunity is real. It is not mandatory reporting—an institution that sees the red flags and stays silent is not liable under Senior Safe for staying silent. But in California, the analysis does not end there. The state's elder financial abuse statute reaches beyond the reporting question. The question is not only whether the firm reported. The question is what the firm did when it saw.

The retired engineer who wired three hundred and forty thousand dollars to Hong Kong had not sent a foreign wire in the previous five years. His bank has a compliance system. The system flags foreign wires. Somebody at the bank reviewed the flag, or did not. Somebody placed a hold, or did not. Somebody called the client to confirm the instruction, or did not.

The widower who sent eight hundred and twenty thousand dollars to a woman in Prague over eleven months sent dozens of wires. His advisor of twenty years processed them. What the advisor asked him, if anything, and what the advisor documented, are questions the advisor's file will answer.

The couple who lost two million dollars to a fabricated cryptocurrency platform moved the money out of accounts the financial advisor had built over four decades. The advisor watched the portfolio deplete. What the advisor said, and when, and to whom, are the questions.

In each case, the professional had information the family did not have. The pattern of the wires. The size relative to normal activity. The destination. The frequency. The age of the client. The advisor was in a position to act. Acting would have meant the call to the client's daughter. The hold under FINRA's exploitation rule. The note in the file that said the client does not wire money overseas and this wire does not sit right. The follow-up when the wires continued.

California elder financial abuse claims against financial institutions turn on a few questions. Was the client an elder or a dependent adult under the statute. Did the institution take, or assist in the taking of, property for a wrongful use. Did the institution know, or should have known, that the conduct was likely to be harmful to the elder. The statute does not require the institution to have run the scam. It requires the institution to have assisted, or to have known and failed to act.

What constitutes assistance is a question of fact. Processing the wire is not, standing alone, enough. Processing the wire after internal flags, after the compliance system generated a review, after a relationship manager noticed the pattern and documented concern, and then did nothing—that is a different case.

The institution's own records typically answer the question. A preservation letter goes early, covering account statements, wire instructions, internal communications, compliance flags, exception reports, notes in the client relationship management system, emails between the advisor and the client, emails within the firm about the client's activity. The letter preserves the record. The record is typically the case.

Recovery from the scammer is rare. Recovery from the institution, where the facts support it, is different. The institution carries insurance. The institution has assets. The institution has reputational exposure the individual perpetrator does not have. California's mandatory fee-shifting and double-damages provisions in elder financial abuse cases reshape the economic calculation in a way that reaches institutional defendants specifically.

None of this means every scam case is a viable claim against the advisor or the bank. Most are not. The ones that are share a pattern: a long-standing advisory relationship, red flags that the firm's own systems identified, a failure to escalate, and a documentary record that shows the failure. When the pattern is present, the case reaches a defendant the family did not know they could reach.

The scammer is unreachable. The question the family asks after is what the professional whose job was to watch should have done, and when.

Three million dollars. The scammer took what he took. The estate is what is left.

Seven

The Structure That Starts the War

She was ninety years old, frail from shingles, and the trustees of her husband's estate would not pay her.

In June 2023, Dianne Feinstein's daughter Katherine filed a petition in San Francisco Superior Court under a limited power of attorney. The allegation was that the trustees of Richard Blum's estate had not funded the marital trust he had established for his widow, had not made the quarterly distributions he had directed, and had not reimbursed her medical expenses—including the shingles hospitalization that had kept her from the Senate that spring.

Fifteen months after Blum's death, none of what he had planned for her had happened.

She died on September 29, 2023. She had never received a distribution from her husband's trust.

What the Plan Said

Richard Blum had been a San Francisco financier whose net worth had at one point exceeded a billion dollars. He had planned carefully. A revocable living trust during his lifetime. A marital trust for Feinstein—a separate structure, funded from his estate, designed to support her for the rest of her life. The documents were not vague. The trustees were directed to fund the marital trust with five million dollars in cash and marketable securities. They were directed to distribute its income to Feinstein in quarterly installments—a minimum of one and a half million dollars annually. If income fell short, they were to make up the difference from principal.

The plan was what a careful estate lawyer would draft for a wealthy man whose widow would outlive him. Specific amounts. Specific intervals. Specific fallbacks. Nothing left to interpretation.

The complaint Katherine filed in June 2023 alleged that the trustees had refused to fund the trust, refused to make distributions, and refused to account.

The Trustees

The trustees were Michael Klein and Marc Scholvinck. Both had been Blum's business associates. Neither had a direct relationship with Feinstein independent of her marriage.

Their response to the lawsuit was that the estate carried a large tax liability and lacked liquidity. Trusts of that size often do. Federal estate tax comes due within nine months of death, and a trustee administering a complex estate may legitimately need time to assess what can be sold and what must be held.

That explanation had a problem.

In the spring of 2023—the same period during which Feinstein was hospitalized, the same period during which her trust remained unfunded—the trustees sold a hotel in Berkeley for a reported one hundred and sixty-three million dollars. The trust Blum had directed be funded with five million dollars was, in the grand scale of the estate, a rounding error. The trustees did not explain why none of those hotel proceeds had been directed to the marital trust. They did not explain why the quarterly distributions had not begun.

What they explained, instead, was that they were working on it.

By August 2023, Katherine Feinstein had filed a third lawsuit. The new complaint alleged financial elder abuse under California law. A San Francisco judge ordered the parties to mediation. The resolution, whatever it was, was not made public. Dianne Feinstein died six weeks later.

What the Structure Cannot Fix

No estate plan can fully eliminate the conflict a marital trust creates. The interests are adverse by construction. Every dollar distributed to the surviving spouse during her lifetime is a dollar that does not pass to the remainder beneficiaries. The structure depends entirely on the trustees.

The deceased spouse knew this when he chose them. In most cases, the choice is a former business partner, a longtime attorney, a friend. Someone the deceased trusted. The structure assumes that trust, once conferred, will honor the dead man's intent.

In the Feinstein-Blum case, the structure did not deliver what the man who designed it had paid for. He had been specific. Five million dollars. Quarterly. A minimum of a million and a half a year. Principal if income fell short. A ninety-year-old woman who had served her country for three decades died before the trustees he had chosen had moved the first dollar.

The relevance of the case is not the scale. I have seen the same pattern—trustees who sat, year after year, on distributions they owed the surviving spouse—in estates of three hundred thousand dollars. The Probate Code does not change based on estate size. What changes is the widow's leverage. A senator's daughter can file three lawsuits in eighteen months. A seventy-nine-year-old widow in Modesto, living on Social Security and the distribution her husband's trust was supposed to be providing, usually cannot. She does not know the trust was not funded. She does not know the trustees have not accounted. She knows the check is not arriving and the trustee's secretary is not returning her calls.

She calls me after the fourth quarter without a distribution. Sometimes after the eighth.

The trust was funded in the document. It was not funded in the bank account. The distance between the two is the case.

The Feinstein case is one face of the structural failure. It is the case where the document was clear and the trustees ignored it.

There is another face. It is the case where the document was followed, to the letter, and the document itself did not hold.

The Words That Didn't Hold

The watches were a collection. The trust called them jewelry.

There were more than eighty-five of them. Some were the kind of watches anyone might call jewelry—a wedding band with a face on it, a gold piece for formal occasions. Some were collector pieces, the kind of thing a wealthy man accumulates when he has a particular interest and forty years of accumulating to do.

When Robin Williams died in August 2014 at his home in Tiburon, the question of which category the watches belonged to was left to a trust his attorney had drafted. The trust used the word "jewelry."

The word was not enough to hold what it was asked to hold.

Four months after Williams's death, his widow Susan Schneider filed a petition in San Francisco Superior Court asking the judge to clarify what the trust meant. Williams's three children—Zachary, Zelda, and Cody—responded that she was trying to rewrite their father's will.

Williams had done what careful estate planners do. After his 2011 marriage to Schneider, his third wife, he had amended his trust to provide for her. The amended plan separated the marital interests from the children's interests. Schneider received the right to live in their Tiburon home for the rest of her life, with a funded reserve to cover its expenses. The children were the primary beneficiaries of the estate, which was estimated at close to one hundred million dollars. His Napa Valley property and its contents were designated for them. The Tiburon home and most of its contents were held for Schneider.

The structure was thoughtful. The separation was clear. The estate had been organized the way a careful man organizes things.

MEMORABILIA

The disputes were specific and, in isolation, almost mundane. They are the reason the chapter exists.

Did the word "memorabilia" include only items related to Williams's acting career—the Academy Award, the props from films, the items he had kept from studios—or did it include everything he had collected over a lifetime? The watch collection alone was estimated in the millions. The question of what counted as "memorabilia" touched dozens of items—props, scripts, photographs, awards, gifts from directors and co-stars accumulated over forty years in the industry.

"Memorabilia" is not a defined legal term. It describes an intuition. In an ordinary estate it does not matter—most people do not own memorabilia in any meaningful sense, and what they do own is modest enough that a dispute about it is not worth the attorney's fees.

In an estate with forty years of film industry accumulation, "memorabilia" is doing massive amounts of work. It is trying to carry a distinction the drafter did not articulate. Is a script memorabilia? What about a script annotated by the director? A prop? A gift from a co-star? A framed photograph with a personal inscription? The attorney drafting the trust had to pick words. The words he picked left the answers to a court.

A San Francisco judge gave the parties until July 2015 to settle. They did. The terms were not fully disclosed, but Schneider's attorneys said she would receive enough support to remain in the Tiburon home, keep some sentimental items—their wedding gifts, selected clothing, a watch Williams often wore, the bicycle they bought together on their honeymoon—and that the children would receive the vast majority of his personal property, including the Academy Award, his remaining watches, and more than fifty bicycles.

Both sides described the outcome as consistent with Williams's wishes. That phrase—consistent with his wishes—is the problem. It required a year of litigation to determine what his wishes had been, for assets he had specifically tried to direct, in a plan he had specifically drafted to prevent this kind of fight.

What Vague Language Does

The trust did not fail because the estate was complicated, though it was. It did not fail because the relationships were bad, though they were strained. It failed because the vocabulary of the distribution did not match the assets being distributed.

The lesson is not that Williams failed to plan. He did plan. The lesson is that in a blended-family estate with significant and varied assets, vague language is a delayed-action mechanism. It does not detonate during the drafter's lifetime. It waits for the death, for the grief, for the first moment when the surviving spouse and the children sit across a conference room table with lawyers. Then it detonates.

In the cases I handle, the Williams pattern recurs in smaller estates without the public record. A blended-family trust is drafted. The drafter uses ordinary words for ordinary categories. The client does not own ordinary categories of property—a family business, a working ranch, a collection of something, a library, a partnership interest that cannot be physically divided. At the client's death, the widow and the children open the document and read the same sentences and reach different conclusions about what they mean.

The sentences are the plan. The plan is what the clients paid for. When the sentences do not hold, the plan does not hold, and the family pays the difference in attorney's fees and years of delay.

Two Faces of the Same Failure

The Feinstein-Blum estate and the Williams estate are not the same case. The first is a story about trustees who refused to follow a plan that was perfectly clear. The second is a story about language that could not bear the weight the plan placed on it. But they share a structure, and the structure is the point.

A careful man looks at his estate and tries to solve the problem the law does not solve cleanly: a second spouse who will outlive him, children from a prior marriage who expect what he has built to come to them in the end, assets that have to support one without being consumed before they pass to the other. He hires a planner. He signs documents. He believes he has done the work.

The documents are then handed to other people.

In the Feinstein case, those people chose not to perform them. In the Williams case, those people performed them exactly, and what they performed was not what the drafter had meant.

Either way, the blended family ends up in court. Either way, the surviving spouse and the children end up paying lawyers to argue about what a dead man intended, with the dead man unavailable to say.

The plan is the sentences. When the sentences do not hold, nothing else does.

For the Reader Who Recognizes This

My late husband's trustees are not paying me what he directed. What can I do?

A California surviving spouse has several remedies under Probate Code § 17200, which governs petitions concerning trust administration. Compel an accounting. Compel distribution. In appropriate cases, petition for the trustee's removal or suspension. Where the withholding rises to the level of financial elder abuse under Welfare and Institutions Code §§ 15610.30 and 15657.7, mandatory attorney's fees on recovery apply, and double damages under Probate Code § 859 are available on a finding of bad faith.

The trust my late parent signed uses words that don't match what they actually owned. Can a California court clarify or correct it?

Yes, through two distinct California procedures. A petition for instructions under Probate Code § 17200(b)(1) asks the court to construe ambiguous trust language. A petition for reformation under Probate Code § 15409 and related authorities asks the court to modify the instrument itself when the language fails to reflect the settlor's actual intent due to a drafting mistake. Reformation requires clear and convincing evidence of the intent.

The family is in a blended-family estate with ambiguous language. Do we have to litigate?

Most California trust-construction disputes settle, often through mediation ordered or encouraged by the probate court. A later chapter describes three such mediations in detail. Litigation remains available when mediation fails, but the settlement rate in these cases is high, and the cost of a settled matter is a fraction of the cost of trial.

More detailed answers appear in the Appendix: Questions and Answers at the end of this book.

EIGHT

WHAT THE RECORD REMEMBERS

She wrote it herself. Four days before the trust was restated. She sent it to her own brother.

Margaret was eighty-four years old, recovering from hip replacement surgery in a house she had lived in for more than thirty years. Her stepdaughter Diane had flown in from out of state to help. On the evening of September 13, 2024, Diane sat in the kitchen and sent a text message to her brother Robert.

She is doing laundry, going through paperwork, literally on speed. I keep telling her to lay down and she won't. She is going to hurt herself and probably shouldn't have had this surgery.

Four days later, Diane drove Margaret to an attorney's office. The existing estate plan—forty percent to Robert, sixty percent to Diane, unchanged for fourteen years—was restated. Robert's share was eliminated. The new trust declared that he was "knowingly and intentionally excluded."

Margaret died the following summer.

Robert's attorney obtained the text thread in discovery. Diane's own words, dated, attributed, sent to the brother whose inheritance she erased four days later.

The text was not written for a courtroom. It was written to a sibling, on an ordinary Friday night, in the kind of language a woman uses when she is tired and worried and alone in someone else's kitchen. *Literally on speed.* The phrase is not legal. It is recognizable. A person who has watched a parent after surgery knows what it means.

The most useful evidence in these cases is almost never the evidence the family produced. It is the evidence the other side produced. The text that went to the sibling. The email that went to the drafting attorney. The voicemail left on an answering machine at a moment of confusion. The record the exploiter did not know she was making.

The Voicemail

Margaret's voice survived her in one recording.

On a Sunday in June 2025—nine months after the restatement, one month before she died—Margaret called Robert's wife. Robert's wife did not pick up. The voicemail ran twenty-two seconds.

This isn't a good time right now. I'm a little confused. Di will be here on the 7th through the 12th. Maybe if you call during that time she can get things straightened out.

She was eighty-five years old. She was calling to say she could not answer her own phone. She was referring her daughter-in-law to her other stepdaughter—the one the trust had just been restated to favor—as the person who could sort things out.

The voicemail was saved. Robert's wife kept it on the phone she replaced that autumn, then on the phone after that. Four minutes of work—a transfer cable, a laptop, a free audio file—and the voicemail outlived Margaret and outlived the phone.

A voicemail like Margaret's is the kind of evidence a forensic expert can use in a capacity reconstruction. Pace, word-finding, the moments where the speaker loses the thread of her own sentence. These are the functional markers that correlate with the medical record. The diagnosis Margaret eventually received—rapidly progressive vascular dementia from a silent stroke no one had identified while she was alive—was the diagnosis the voicemail was already describing.

Margaret had not known she was creating a record. She was calling to apologize for not being able to answer her own phone. The record was a byproduct of her effort to stay in touch with people she loved.

Those are often the strongest records the families have.

The Letter That Was Never Mailed

On July 4, 2025, Margaret sat down at her kitchen table and wrote a letter to Robert.

It ran two pages. Her handwriting—which had been even and readable for decades—was loose and crabbed and in places ran off the line. The letter said she loved him. It said she was sorry. It said she did not remember signing what Diane had told her she had signed. It said she wanted to see him.

She put the letter in an envelope. She wrote his address. She did not put a stamp on it.

The envelope sat on the kitchen counter for ten days and then migrated, in the way that papers migrate in a house where the person living in it is forgetting what she meant to do, to a stack of opened mail in the hallway. It stayed there through

Margaret's final decline in mid-July. It was still there when the paramedics came.

Robert did not find the letter until September, eight weeks after his stepmother's death, when he was clearing the house with his wife and son. It was in a stack of unopened condolence cards that a neighbor had been gathering from the mailbox after the funeral.

The letter is not admissible as testamentary intent under California law. It was not executed with the formalities of a will or a trust amendment. It does not change what is in the restated document.

The letter is evidence of capacity. It is evidence of state of mind. It is evidence that on a Friday in July, ten days before she died, Margaret did not believe she had disinherited her stepson. She thought a conversation was still possible. She thought she had time.

The handwriting itself carried evidence the words did not. A letter written by a woman whose hand had been steady for decades, and was no longer steady, is the kind of document a forensic document examiner can read. The tremor that was not there five years earlier. The drifting line. The moments where the pen lifted and returned in a different place. Vascular dementia on paper. The same disease the silent stroke had caused. The same disease no one had diagnosed while she was still alive to be treated.

Margaret did not intend to leave a record. She intended to mail a letter. The record is what she left because the letter did not get mailed.

The Date on the Death Certificate

Eleanor was eighty-one years old and dying of Alzheimer's disease in an Alameda County hospital.

Her daughter Catherine had been her caregiver for most of the previous year. On July 7, Catherine brought an attorney to the hospital room. A durable power of attorney was executed. Seven days later—on July 14—Catherine brought the attorney back. A complete restatement of Eleanor's trust was signed. The restatement redirected the estate to Catherine and eliminated Eleanor's other children, who had been named beneficiaries for years.

Eleanor died on July 21.

Her death certificate listed Alzheimer's disease as the cause of death.

The trust restatement was dated seven days earlier than the death certificate. The power of attorney was dated fourteen days earlier. Both documents, and the certificate, sat in a county filing system that anyone with a name and a date could search.

There was no text message in Eleanor's case. There was no voicemail. There was no unmailed letter. What there was was an arithmetic problem.

A California court asked to assess whether a woman with a terminal cognitive disease understood what she was signing fourteen days before her death does not need the sibling's text or the neighbor's observation. The court needs the two dates. It needs the attorney's file. It needs the hospital record of what Eleanor could and could not do in the week the documents were signed.

The attorney had prepared the power of attorney and then, seven days later, the full trust restatement. The hospital record for those two weeks—vitals, medication orders, nurse's notes, dietary intake, consulting physician visits—existed in a form that could not be altered after the fact. The attorney's file existed in a form that became available on Eleanor's death, under the testamentary exception to the attorney-client privilege, to any party claiming through the deceased client.

Eleanor's children had no private evidence to produce. They were not in the hospital room. They did not see their mother's condition on July 14. What they had was a death certificate they could order from the county and a trust document the trustee was required to produce.

The distance between the two dates was the case.

Most of the work in a contested restatement-before-death case is not finding new evidence. It is asking the documentary record that already exists to speak in the order the events actually occurred. The hospital's records. The attorney's calendar. The notary's logbook. The family's understanding of what the decedent could do in the final two weeks, measured against what the documents say she did.

The death certificate does not decide a trust contest. The hospital record does not decide it. The attorney's file does not decide it.

The three of them, laid next to one another on the timeline, usually do.

THOMAS

There was a third record, briefer than Margaret's and narrower than Eleanor's. It belonged to a man from the first chapter of this book.

Thomas was sixty-three. He had been drinking heavily for most of his adult life. On October 18, 2024, eight days after he left a Napa rehab program against medical advice, his attorney walked him through a trust amendment that redirected assets away from his wife and son.

His wife later obtained his phone.

During the meeting with the attorney, Thomas had been texting her. The messages were time-stamped to the minute.

I'm on drugs. I can't drive.

There are goblins in the corner.

The attorney had been Thomas's estate planner for thirty-five years. His file for the October 18 signing—obtained after Thomas's death through discovery—contained no note about the client's condition. No capacity assessment. No recommendation for independent review. The attorney had notarized the amendment and gone home.

Thomas's blood alcohol at the time of his death, nine months later, was three times the legal limit.

Three records. The texts from the signing. The attorney's file, silent in a way the silence itself recorded. The toxicology report attached to the death certificate.

None of the three was produced by anyone trying to build a case. Thomas was texting his wife. The attorney was following a routine he had followed for decades. The coroner was filling out a form.

The case that followed his death was built on the three of them laid in sequence.

The Record

None of them was building a case.

Margaret was texting her daughter-in-law that she was confused. Eleanor was dying of a disease no one was going to cure. Thomas was texting his wife from a conference room he could not fully track.

The exploiters around them chose moments. They did not choose what got recorded around the moments.

A family that has lost a parent often believes the case depends on what they themselves remember. What they saw at Thanksgiving. What their sibling said on the phone.

Memory matters. It is not usually what the case turns on.

The case turns on what was already being written while the family was trying to understand what it was watching.

Margaret is buried next to her husband outside San Jose. Eleanor is buried in Alameda County. Thomas's ashes are in a Sierra cabin his wife kept.

The records they left are in phones, in files, in county databases none of the three of them thought about.

The silence around them is what died.

Nine

The Window

Her cousin flew up from Los Angeles that morning. He'd been a lawyer at an Am Law 50 firm before he retired, and he knew what he was looking at.

The call came on a Tuesday in November. Graham had spent the weekend reading a document his cousin's widow had been asked to sign. The successor trustee named in the existing trust was Graham himself. When he asked to see the instrument, the other lawyer told him it would be illegal to share it.

That is not how trust law works. A named successor trustee has every right to see the document. Graham had spent forty years in courtrooms. He recognized the lie in a sentence.

He called me within the week.

I assembled the team. A California-licensed independent fiduciary. A licensed private investigator. Later, an estate planning attorney to inventory the documents. We met at Helena's house in Woodside.

Graham was there when I arrived. He had flown up from LAX on the early flight and driven straight from the airport. He stood by the window with his arms crossed, watching the driveway. Gray suit, no tie. When I came in, he shook my hand and said nothing. He didn't need to. His face said it all —the quiet fury of a man who had spent forty years in courtrooms and knew exactly what had been done to his cousin's widow.

Helena sat in the living room in an elegant blue pantsuit. Pearls. Diamond rings. White hair pulled back. Her hands rested in her lap, still.

She had come to California from Leeds when she was nineteen. Arrived with a suitcase and an accent she never fully lost. Built a company with her husband over four decades. Hundreds of employees at its peak. She had managed payroll, negotiated contracts, and handled problems that would have broken most people. The immigrant's determination to make something of herself in a new country—she had done it.

Now she sat in her own living room, embarrassed.

I'm a businesswoman, she said. The accent still there, softened by decades. I built a company. I negotiated with people who tried to cheat me for forty years. I don't understand how this could have happened to me.

She paused. Looked at her hands.

If this can happen, what else can happen?

The scheme was sophisticated. Multiple trust amendments over three years. Each one shifted more control to the new trustees, more assets to new beneficiaries. Charitable giving that had defined Helena's values—eliminated. Family members systematically removed.

Then the manufactured crisis. Two doctors, coordinated opinions, both reaching the same conclusion within weeks:

Helena lacked capacity. The new trustee assumed control. He planned to withdraw half a million dollars from her accounts.

We did not announce ourselves. I knew the opposing lawyer. He knew me. I was not sure yet how much he understood about what his clients were doing. Either way, surprise was our only advantage.

We hit them from three directions at once.

First, the revocation. Helena's trust contained a provision the scheme had overlooked: the settlor could revoke the instrument at any time by written document. No physician approval required. The scheme had been built on incapacity provisions —but incapacity governs trustee succession, not the settlor's fundamental right to revoke.

Two different doors in the same document. They had locked the wrong one.

On a gray morning in mid-November, Helena signed the revocation. Every amendment made during her years of vulnerability—collapsed in a single stroke. The new trustee's authority vanished.

Second, the freeze. Letters went to every bank, brokerage, and investment advisor holding Helena's assets. Immediate cessation of all trustee activities. Restore full account access to the settlor. Remove the new trustee from any signatory authority. Cease honoring any of his requests.

Third, notice to the professionals. Tax advisors. Registered investment advisors. Financial planners. Everyone who might execute a transfer now knew the trustee's authority was contested.

The revocation alone would not have stopped them if the accounts were already drained. The freeze alone would not have mattered if the trustee still had legal authority. The notices alone would have been ignored without the other two.

Together, they collapsed the scheme before anyone could react.

The half million dollars never moved.

If Graham had accepted the lawyer's refusal. If he had waited another week to call me. If I had sent the letters one at a time instead of all at once. The margin was that thin.

Once the other side saw my name on the letters, they knew they had a problem. Their carefully constructed authority had evaporated. The accounts were frozen. The professionals were on notice. Fighting would cost them more than retreating.

One of the alleged perpetrators turned over documents voluntarily—boxes of files delivered to Helena's house without a subpoena. I have seen it before. Schemes hold together when everyone believes they will win. When that belief cracks, someone decides to be on the right side of what is coming. The delivery told me more than the documents inside.

We obtained an independent psychiatric evaluation from a board-certified geriatric specialist. His conclusion: Helena possessed testamentary capacity. Her desire to revoke the amendments was consistent, rational, and reflected restored decisional autonomy.

The manufactured incapacity findings collapsed under the weight of a real evaluation.

Helena still lives in Woodside. Her accounts are her own. Her estate plan reflects her actual wishes. The people who tried to take everything from her got nothing.

A long way from Leeds.

Graham called on a Tuesday. By the following Friday, the revocation was signed and the accounts were frozen.

Seven days.

Kate's call came on a Thursday in October.

The document had been signed four years earlier. Her

mother Frances had been eighty years old at the time. She was eighty-three now. She lived in the Pasadena house she and her husband had bought in 1978. Her husband had died nine years ago. She had four adult children. The one she trusted most was her son Daniel.

Daniel was a financial advisor with his own practice. He had managed Frances's taxes, her investments, and her retirement accounts for most of her adult life. When Frances had a question about money, Daniel was the person she called.

In February of the year she turned eighty, Frances signed an irrevocable trust. The document had been prepared by an attorney Daniel used for his own practice. Frances had no independent counsel. Daniel drove her to the signing. The notary met them at his office.

Frances believed she was making Daniel executor of her estate. The document did something else. It transferred her primary residence—the Pasadena house—into an irrevocable trust naming Daniel as sole trustee and sole beneficiary. He received all income from the trust, quarterly, mandatory. He held an unlimited right to withdraw the principal at any time. Upon Frances's death, he could direct the remaining assets to anyone, including his own creditors.

Frances retained nothing. She could not amend the trust. She could not revoke it. She could not serve as trustee. She remained liable, however, for the income taxes on trust property, because the document had been drafted as a grantor trust for federal tax purposes.

She also lost her Proposition 13 basis. The house she had lived in for more than forty years carried a property tax assessment from 1978. The transfer to Daniel's irrevocable trust ended it. Going forward, the property would be assessed at current market value.

None of this was explained to her.

Kate discovered the trust two years after her mother signed it. She asked Frances about the document. Frances said Daniel had become her executor.

Kate asked to see the document. Daniel said it was not necessary for her to see it. Frances had a copy. He did not need to show anyone anything. Kate's brother found the recorded grant deed online.

It took another two years before Kate could get her mother in front of an independent attorney. Frances refused, then agreed, then canceled, then agreed again. The appointment happened on a Wednesday in July. The attorney read the document aloud and explained what it did. Frances sat with her hands folded in her lap. When he finished, she asked him to explain it again.

Kate recorded the meeting on her phone. I have listened to it. Frances's voice is clear. When she understands what she has signed, she does not cry. She says, very quietly, *I did not mean to do that.*

That recording should have been the case.

It was not.

An irrevocable trust is difficult to unwind. The statutory presumption that applies to transfers drafted by care custodians or attorneys does not apply to transfers to blood relatives. A son who is also a financial advisor is still a son.

To dismantle the trust, Frances would need to bring an action. The recording, the drafter's conflict, the absence of independent counsel, the pattern across properties—the case had the elements. But it needed Frances, as petitioner, to pursue it.

Frances was eighty-three. Her capacity was intact but it was not steady.

On a Tuesday morning in November, she told Kate she wanted to fight. She had been sick over the weekend and thinking about her life and she was angry about what Daniel had done. She told Kate to call the attorney. To do whatever it takes.

On Thursday afternoon, she told Kate she did not want to upset Daniel. He was her son. He had always taken care of her. She was sure there had been a misunderstanding. She asked Kate not to make trouble.

On Sunday she did not remember either conversation. She asked Kate how her week had been.

That was the pattern.

The law recognizes two states of mind—capacity and incapacity. A person either possesses the ability to understand the nature and consequences of her decisions, or she does not. Frances possessed that ability. On any given afternoon, shown the trust document and asked what it did, she could explain it. She could explain what she had signed and what she had not understood at the time. She could explain what she wanted done about it.

What she could not do was hold the decision.

Kate sent me the recording in October. She called me in November after her mother's third reversal. A lawsuit would take eighteen months at minimum. Depositions. Discovery. Experts. Trial. Every stage would require Frances's participation. Every stage would require her to hold, for weeks at a time, a position she could not hold for forty-eight hours.

Daniel's counsel would see the pattern within the first month. Every Tuesday the case would advance. Every Thursday Frances would call her son, apologize, and tell him she did not want to proceed. By the time of her deposition, she would be a sympathetic but impossible witness. Daniel's lawyer would not need to attack her. He would only need to ask her, on cross-examination, whether she loved her son. She would say yes. He would ask whether she wanted to take back the gift she had made to him. She might say yes. She might say no. She might say she did not remember making any gift.

The recording would come in. It would not be enough. A woman who could not sustain her own claim for a week could not sustain it through discovery, trial, and appeal.

Kate asked what else I could do.

The legal tools are not missing. They exist. What is missing is the principal. The law requires a principal who can direct counsel. Counsel cannot direct the principal. That is the rule, and it is the rule for reasons I have never wished were otherwise.

Frances is still alive. The house is still titled to Daniel's trust. He has not exercised his withdrawal right, and Frances is still living there, but nothing in the document requires him to let her stay. He pays the property taxes now, at the current assessed value. She reports the grantor-trust income on her returns and pays the federal tax on money she does not receive.

She declines, slowly. Kate calls every day. Her brother calls twice a week. They do not bring up the trust anymore. It upsets Frances, and when she is upset she gets confused, and when she is confused the decline accelerates.

Helena had seven days.

Frances has had four years.

The tools are on the table. They have been on the table since Kate called. They will still be on the table tomorrow.

The hand that has to reach for them is not steady.

Kate keeps the recording on her phone, in a folder she does not open.

Ten

How Cases End: Three Mediations

Four Hours

December morning. Fog on the highway east. The sun not up yet.

I got to the office early. Reread the high points of the brief.

George had been eighty-two when he died. Lived alone. COPD, lung cancer, diabetes. Expressive aphasia—couldn't get complex thoughts out. Poor short-term memory. Wheelchair-bound at the end.

Claire had been his caregiver for three years. Drove him everywhere. Managed his medications. Became his healthcare surrogate. Then, five months after the family ranch sold, she became the sole beneficiary of his Fidelity account.

His sister Anne was his only heir. He died intestate. Claire never told Anne her brother had died. His body sat in the morgue until Anne found out on her own.

The account held $3 million—$2.6 million in securities and

bonds, $400,000 cash. Fidelity had locked it before we even filed the lawsuit. Three million dollars frozen. No access. There but not there.

Ten o'clock. I turned on Zoom.

The boxes appeared. Peter Wright from San Francisco, twenty-sixth floor, white shirt and plaid wool sportcoat for the winter cold. David Hale in his office across the river. Anne from England—six in the evening there, dressed for cold English winter but inside her warm home, her husband's voice somewhere off camera. And Patricia, the mediator, from Los Angeles —professional look, thirty years in trust and estate disputes.

I had on a white shirt, no tie, blue corduroy sportcoat.

Claire and her lawyers were somewhere in southern California. The investment advisor somewhere else. We would never see them. Not even a blank screen. Patricia shuttled between separate Zooms—they couldn't see or hear us, we couldn't see or hear them. Just Patricia, carrying numbers back and forth.

Patricia did the small talk first. Asked Anne about the time difference. Then the speech—confidentiality, voluntary process, anything said in caucus stays confidential.

She asked for our opening.

Peter spoke. "Our opening is we sued them for the return of $3 million. That's our opening."

Patricia smiled. "They know that. Maybe start with something different."

"Ninety-five percent to our client," Peter said. "Five percent to Claire."

Patricia nodded. Disappeared into the other room.

Twenty minutes. We waited. My hands on the desk.

When Patricia came back, she had the number: $3 million. Claire was on the call with her lawyers and an investment advisor named Grace who claimed she'd had frequent calls with

George. Grace wasn't present when the beneficiary form was signed.

Their opening: 95/5. The mirror.

The numbers moved. 90/10. They mirrored. Around noon they broke pattern—84/16. We came back. They came back at 75/25.

Their lawyer sent a message through Patricia. "We're running out of runway."

"If that's true," I said, "let's quit now and litigate for the next two years. We're here to settle today."

Patricia went back.

I shifted from percentages to dollars. $900,000 for Claire. They rejected it. Came back with the same figure—but to Anne.

We went to $1 million for Claire.

At a million dollars, I knew. She would become a millionaire in that meeting. Today. They would settle.

They mirrored. $1.2 million for Claire. They mirrored again.

We were $300,000 apart. Half the account was $1.5 million.

I told Patricia it was time to go 50/50.

Their lawyer protested. "This is not a 50/50 case."

It was.

They agreed.

David documented the deal. Two fifteen in the afternoon.

I looked at Anne's face on the screen. Four hours, and it was done.

"Thank you," she said. Her voice steady. "Thank you for getting this done."

$1.5 million to Anne. $1.5 million to Claire—who hadn't told Anne her brother died, who'd left his body in the morgue.

The Zoom boxes closed one by one.

4,000 SHARES

September afternoon. Warm. I left the office at four for the drive south.

Ninety miles. I stopped at a steakhouse I always stop at—steak before mediation, a habit now. Forty-one miles left. The hotel. I checked in and slept.

Morning. Breakfast at the hotel—protein for the day. Four-minute drive to the mediation center. Starched Levis, white shirt, blue corduroy coat.

Colonel Henry Arthur Grant died in March at ninety-two. Born in South Carolina in 1932. West Point graduate. Career Army. A man who followed orders and gave them. When he died, they buried him at the Military Academy cemetery. Back where he started.

His wife Martha was already gone. They'd left a trust worth five million dollars. Their daughter Diana got distributions for life—health, education, maintenance, support. Their granddaughter Sarah, my client, got half the remainder when Diana died. Matthew, Diana's son, got the other half.

The problem was time. Diana was sixty-three and healthy. She might live another thirty years. Matthew would be in his sixties before he saw a dollar. Sarah would wait just as long. The trust would grow fat—six percent a year, compounding—while the trustee's fees bled it and everyone aged.

Sarah lives in Iowa. Twenty-nine years old. Her mother died young. Diana is her aunt. Her husband has failing kidneys. They have twin boys. She may be the sole income provider for her family. Money thirty years from now doesn't help raise her children. It doesn't help now.

The corporate trustee named in the trust had declined to serve. That left the beneficiaries to appoint someone new.

Which meant they had to agree. Which meant they had to talk.

Diana's lawyer told Sarah she needed her own counsel. She found me.

They'd offered her five hundred thousand and a share of a house that might take a year to sell. No lawyer. No leverage. Just a number and a suggestion to sign.

I got a copy of the trust. Read every page. Then I got a copy of the trust assets—the Fidelity statements, the stock positions, the cash. I input them into a tracking portfolio. Watched them every day. I knew what they had. I knew what it was worth. I knew how it moved.

The standard advice for an irrevocable trust is to petition the court. The court can modify the trust—but only if the modification doesn't defeat a material purpose. That's the trap. A judge reads a trust the way the dead wrote it.

But you practice long enough, you learn to read differently. You stop looking for what the law allows you to do to a trust. You start looking for what the trust allows you to do with itself.

The Grants had built a door. They just didn't know they'd built it.

The corporate trustee had declined. The beneficiaries could appoint a new trustee—if they agreed. The trustee had discretion to distribute principal. Any dispute about how to exercise that discretion could be resolved through mediation. The trust itself allowed it.

We didn't need to modify the trust. We didn't need to petition the court. We needed to use what the Grants gave us.

I have read hundreds of trusts. Maybe thousands. You hold the pages and you know the person who signed them is gone. Their hand moved across the signature line. They thought they were done. They thought they had settled everything—who gets what, when, how. They couldn't know what would happen after. What their children would need. What their grandchildren would face. They couldn't know their words would still be issuing orders decades later, from the grave.

But sometimes, in the words themselves, there's a way out. The dead write more than they know. The Colonel—the West Point man, the officer who followed orders—had written instructions that could free his family from the very structure he'd built.

The trust itself was the door.

Friendly reception at the mediation center. Large conference rooms with video setups. I got one to myself. The mediator came in to greet me—business attire, well dressed. A retired judge, twenty-five years on the bench. She holds herself with dignity but not pride. Loves to settle cases. She's seen it all.

Everyone else appeared on Zoom. Diana's lawyer. Sarah from Iowa—afternoon there, warm in her living room. The proposed trustee, called in to effectuate whatever we agreed.

The mediator assembled us into one meeting. Then she gave the speech.

She'd given it a hundred times. The cost of litigation. She knew the numbers by heart—pre-trial preparation, court days, motions, discovery, depositions, experts, accountants. Each figure landing like a weight on the scale.

Half a million to a million dollars. Two years. Three if someone appeals. And at the end, a judge who reads the trust and says: it means what it says.

Or settle today.

We started at 1.4 million.

They said they thought we'd take nine hundred thousand. Then offered seven hundred.

I knew a million was there.

The portfolio. I'd been watching it for months. I knew the positions. I knew the prices. Apple was trading around two hundred fifty a share. The trust held 4,000 shares. One million dollars exactly.

If the trustee transferred stock instead of cash, he wouldn't have to liquidate anything. No sale. No capital gains event. Clean. Fast. The shares move from one account to another. Done.

We went back and forth. Four hours.

At a million dollars in Apple stock, they agreed.

Two more hours to document the deal. New trustee appointed. Sarah relinquishes her remainder interest—all claims, all future distributions, all standing as a beneficiary. The 4,000 shares transfer within fifteen days. The rest of the trust—four million dollars—goes to Diana. She can keep it. She can share it with Matthew. She can do whatever she wants. No more HEMS restrictions. No more trustee oversight. No more waiting thirty years.

I looked at Sarah's face on the screen. Smile. Relief.

"I can breathe now," she said. "We can breathe."

Sarah came in with an uncertain half-million and minimal house sale proceeds she might see in a year. She left with Apple stock worth a million dollars. Immediate. Liquid. Hers. Money to raise her boys. Money now, when it matters.

Diana and Matthew got four million dollars and their freedom.

Everyone got out. The trust did what the Colonel never knew it could do.

I drove home. Warm evening. Home in time for dinner.

THE ATMOSPHERIC RIVER

November morning. Rain on the windshield, heavy and steady. An atmospheric river had moved in overnight—the kind that floods the Valley, backs up the rivers, turns everything gray for days.

I drove west. Eight miles in heavy rain. Black overcoat on the passenger seat. Starched Levis, white shirt, blue sportcoat.

Francis O'Connor died in May at ninety-three. His wife Kathleen had been gone since 2017. After that, Francis lived alone in a duplex on Callum Street. His son Liam looked after him. New lights. Kitchen repairs. Cleanup when cleanup was needed. The work a son does.

Liam had grown up in that neighborhood. Knew the neighbors. Knew the streets. He'd learned to work on cars in that driveway, his father beside him with grease on his hands, teaching him to change oil, replace brake pads, the practical knowledge that got Liam through thirty years of keeping trucks running. The duplex on Callum Street had been his home for years before his father needed him there. It mattered to him. Not just the money. The place.

In 2019, Francis wrote three documents he called codicils. The first named Liam executor. The second divided the properties—Callum Street to Liam, Ethan Way to his daughter Niamh. The third, eight months later, gave Liam both.

Signed. Dated. Specific about who got what. But not witnessed. California requires two witnesses present at the signing. Francis had none.

When Francis died, Niamh became trustee. Liam went to see a lawyer—a firm prominent in trust litigation. They quoted him thirty-five thousand dollars up front to take the case. He didn't have it. Retired truck driver. No pile of cash sitting around. But they knew me, knew I took complex cases on contingency. They gave him my name.

Liam came to my office with nothing on the table. Zero. Niamh's position was that the codicils were invalid and the original trust terms governed. Under those terms, Liam had no special claim to either property.

I got a copy of the trust. Read every page. Then I went to my library.

The trust gave the surviving spouse a power of appointment—the right to redirect assets if he referenced it specifically. Francis never used those words. He just wrote that Liam should receive the properties.

Two doctrines compete: follow the letter of the requirement, or follow the intent. Courts have gone both ways. The case could settle, or it could drag on for years with an uncertain outcome.

The theory took real thinking. But once I saw it, I knew it raised something the other side couldn't ignore: the prospect of losing completely. If a court applied substantial compliance, Niamh could end up with nothing.

The properties together: $1.1 million. Litigation to trial: $100,000 to $150,000 per side. Two years. Maybe three with appeals.

I told Liam my terms. Forty percent if it goes to mediation, settlement conference, or trial. He pays nothing up front. We both start at zero. If we recover nothing, I get nothing.

He agreed.

I parked in the lot. Rain still coming down.

The conference room doubled as a law library—shelves lined with books and periodicals twenty-five years old. Remnants from before electronic research made paper obsolete. A table with two seats on each side, one at each end.

Liam sat near the door. Workboots, khakis, blue sweater. No overcoat. He'd driven in from north of town through the same rain.

I sat across from him, near the window.

The mediator came in. Stocky build, blue suit, blue-green tie. Thirty-five years in trusts and estates.

Niamh and her lawyer were in the next room. The lawyer in gray suit and black tie, Niamh on Zoom with him. I never saw her. Just the lawyer, when we passed in the hallway.

I gave my opening. Calm, matter of fact. The power of appointment theory. Three codicils over eight months, identifying properties by address, naming recipients by name. The trust didn't require witness formalities for exercising the power. What could be more specific than what Francis wrote?

The mediator listened. Went to the other room.

We waited. Rain against the windows. Liam talked about his father. Francis had been a strong man. Knew what he wanted. Independent his whole life. When he became enfeebled, it embarrassed him. Tough for a man like that. Liam talked about growing up on those streets—the families he knew, the neighbors who'd watched him become a man. About the years driving trucks, the long hauls across the country, coming home. About going back to help his dad when his dad couldn't manage alone. Francis wanted him to have the duplex. Wrote it down four times.

The mediator came back. Went to the other room again. Came back. Three times, four times. The numbers moved. The positions shifted.

I told the mediator what to tell them: we don't want to be hogs. Just half. One property each. What Francis wrote in his second codicil, before he changed his mind, before he gave Liam everything.

Niamh wanted to settle with her brother. No accusations. No attacks. Collegial.

The turn came when the mediator agreed with me on the power of appointment—not the Third Codicil giving Liam both properties, but the Second. January 23, 2019. Callum Street to Liam. Ethan Way to Niamh. If that document validly exercised the power, each sibling got one property.

We worked out the rest. Liam takes the Callum Street duplex—his father's home, where he'd done the repairs. His home too, the place he'd grown up, the neighborhood he knew. Niamh takes Ethan Way. The liquid assets adjusted: Niamh's sixty percent reduced to forty, twenty percent to Liam. The grandchildren keep their shares.

By late afternoon we had it documented.

Liam stood. Walked out to the parking lot without an overcoat. Rain still falling. Rush hour now—headlights on wet pavement. He got in his truck and pulled out, north toward home.

I drove east through the rain.

Eleven

The Justice Gap

The phone rings forty times a week. Sometimes more.

A daughter in Oregon. Her mother died six months ago. The caregiver changed the trust two weeks before the end. The daughter has the documents. She has the medical records. She has a story that would make a jury weep.

She does not have a hundred and fifty thousand dollars.

A son in the Central Valley. His stepmother locked him out of the family home the day after the funeral. His father's will left everything to the children. The new trust—signed when his father could barely hold a pen—leaves everything to her. The son works for the county. He makes sixty-two thousand a year.

A widow in San Diego. Her late husband's business partner drained the accounts while she was in the hospital. She has bank statements showing the transfers. She has a case. She does not have a lawyer.

Fifteen hundred to two thousand inquiries a year reach my office. We accept three to four percent of them.

That is not a statistic. That is a waiting room full of people I cannot help.

What It Costs

Trust and estate litigation is among the most expensive areas of civil law. Most people do not know this until they need it.

A moderately complex trust challenge—single settlor, two beneficiaries, allegations of undue influence, one expert on testamentary capacity—will cost seventy-five to a hundred and fifty thousand dollars per side before anyone sees a courtroom. If the case goes to trial, a one-week trial adds another fifty to a hundred thousand. Summary judgment motions and contested discovery can push the total past two hundred and fifty thousand dollars. Per side.

These are not unusual numbers. They are the ordinary cost of this kind of litigation.

And here is the detail that most families do not learn until it is too late: the trust proponent—the person who benefited from the suspect changes—often pays their attorneys from the trust itself. They are spending the inheritance to defend against the challenge to the inheritance.

The daughter in Oregon. The son in the Central Valley. The widow in San Diego. They are fighting with their own money. The other side is fighting with theirs.

The National Picture

This is not a problem confined to elder abuse cases. It is not confined to any one state.

In three-quarters of civil cases in state courts, at least one party has no lawyer. The Legal Services Corporation's most recent Justice Gap Report found that ninety-two percent of the civil legal problems of low-income Americans received no legal help or inadequate help.

But the crisis extends beyond the poor. Middle-class Americans—families with houses and retirement accounts and jobs—increasingly cannot afford to litigate. They earn too much to qualify for legal aid. They earn too little to fund a lawsuit. The son in the Central Valley makes sixty-two thousand a year. The average cost of taking his case through trial would consume four years of his salary. The justice gap is not just a gap at the bottom. It runs through the middle of American life.

Now apply those numbers to a family that just lost a parent and suspects the trust was changed under undue influence. They are grieving. They are confused. They have a hundred and twenty days from the date of the required notice to file a contest. Miss that deadline, and the claim is gone forever.

The Surgeon and the Waiting Room

My firm handles forty to fifty active cases at any given time. We work on contingency—we collect our fees only if we achieve a recovery.

The contingency model exists because most families in these disputes cannot sustain hourly-rate litigation. A woman whose caregiver drained her accounts does not have thirty-five thousand dollars for a retainer. A disinherited son working for the county does not have two hundred thousand for a trial. The contingency arrangement makes it possible for them to fight at all.

But a contingency case requires that the expected recovery

substantially exceed the cost of getting there. A hundred to three hundred thousand dollars in attorney time and hard costs must come from somewhere. If the estate is too small or the assets are unreachable, the math does not work. Not for the client. Not for the firm.

It is not unlike what happens at a major medical center. The expertise that draws patients from across the state is the same expertise that limits availability. A noted surgeon cannot operate on every patient who seeks care. There must be a process to identify the cases where that expertise can make the greatest difference.

The same is true in this practice. With fifteen hundred to two thousand new inquiries a year—many accompanied by hundreds of pages of trust documents, medical records, financial statements, and correspondence—the volume far exceeds what any single attorney or any one firm can take on.

I wish it were otherwise.

What We Look For

When we evaluate a case for contingency representation, the questions are straightforward.

Is there credible evidence of undue influence, lack of capacity, fraud, or elder financial abuse? Is the estate large enough to justify the cost of litigation? Are the assets identifiable and reachable—because a judgment against an empty trust is worthless? Are we within the applicable statutes of limitation? Are there medical records, financial documents, witness accounts, or communications that support the claim?

If any one fails, the case does not meet the threshold. Not because the caller does not have a grievance. Many do. But because the economics of contingency litigation require a certain alignment of facts, assets, and timing that most cases—through no fault of the family—do not possess.

THE NINETY-SIX PERCENT

What happens to the other ninety-six percent?

Some will find attorneys who handle these matters on an hourly basis. If they can afford it, that may be the right path. Some will consult with multiple firms and hear the same thing we told them—strong case, wrong economics. Some will try to represent themselves. A few will succeed.

Most will do nothing.

They will watch the trust distribute assets to the wrong people. They will carry the knowledge that their parent was exploited and that the legal system could not help them. Some will be angry at the system. Some will be angry at lawyers. Some will simply be tired.

I have thought about this for a long time.

The chapter on mediation describes how most of the cases I handle end in negotiated resolution—families in separate rooms, a neutral mediator shuttling between them, hours of negotiation over what a deceased parent meant when they signed documents that can no longer be amended. Those are the cases that made it through. The families who found a lawyer. Who had a case that justified the cost. Who reached the room where resolution happens.

WHY THIS BOOK EXISTS

I write this book because I believe that understanding how elder financial abuse works—the methods, the tactics, the warning signs—can help families protect themselves before the damage is done.

But I understand now, after fifty years of this work, that a book like this serves another purpose I did not fully anticipate.

For the families who will never retain a contingency lawyer —because the estate is too small, because the assets are gone, because the statute ran—a book may be the most useful thing they encounter. Not because it replaces legal representation. Nothing does. But because understanding the landscape—how undue influence operates, what trustees owe, how capacity is assessed, what mediation looks like, what litigation actually costs—gives families the information they need to make decisions. Real decisions. Not decisions born of ignorance or false hope.

The son in the Central Valley may read a chapter and understand what he is facing—the cost, the timeline, the emotional toll—and decide whether to proceed.

The widow in San Diego may learn enough about elder financial abuse statutes to know what to tell the next attorney she calls.

The daughter in Oregon may recognize, early enough, that her mother's caregiver is isolating her. She may act before the trust is changed. She may never need a lawyer at all.

Knowledge is not justice. But it is the next best thing.

The phone will ring again tomorrow. A family in crisis. Documents they do not understand. A deadline they did not know existed. Someone they trusted who turned out to be someone else.

Forty calls a week. I can take maybe one.

Six o'clock. Enough time to get home for family dinner. I click the sleep button on the MacBook, straighten the desk, turn out my office light. Down the hall. Lights off. Door closed for the night.

I get in my car.

The workday behind me.

For the Reader Who Recognizes This

My case is real but the estate is small. Is there anything I can do?

Yes, and often more than the reader of this chapter thinks. Small-estate cases do not meet the economics of most contingency firms, but several other paths exist. Some California attorneys handle small-estate matters on reduced hourly rates. Legal aid organizations handle some elder-abuse cases where the family qualifies. The State Bar of California Lawyer Referral Service connects families to attorneys willing to conduct limited-scope consultations at modest fees. A single consultation—sometimes free, sometimes a few hundred dollars—will tell you which paths apply to your specific facts. Do not assume nothing is available without asking.

What does a free or low-cost initial consultation with a California trust attorney actually cover?

A competent initial consultation should cover: whether the facts you describe support a claim, which California statutes of limitation apply to which claims, what preservation steps need to happen immediately, and a candid assessment of whether the case is economic to pursue and in what form. A consultation that ends with only a quote for a retainer and no substantive assessment of the case is a consultation that did not do its job. Consultations with experienced California trust and elder abuse counsel are typically 45 to 60 minutes and will give you a working understanding of your situation even if no engagement follows.

If I cannot afford to litigate, what is the most useful thing I can do with what I know?

Three things. Document and preserve everything—Chapter Six describes how. Report the abuse to California Adult Protective Services in the relevant county, and if the exploitation involved wire fraud, cryptocurrency, or online schemes, to the FBI's Internet Crime Complaint Center at ic3.gov. Use what you have learned from this book to protect others in your family—a surviving parent, an aging relative, a sibling. The patterns repeat. Recognition, early, is often the most consequential intervention available. Knowledge does not recover the estate that was lost. It protects the one that has not yet been taken.

More detailed answers appear in the Appendix: Questions and Answers at the end of this book.

Appendix: Questions And Answers

California Law on Trust and Estate Exploitation

This appendix answers the questions families actually ask in the weeks after they discover a parent's estate has been redirected. The answers reflect California law as it stands at the time of this book's publication. California statutes are revised periodically, and a reader planning to act on any answer here should verify the current text with counsel licensed in California. None of what follows is a substitute for legal advice tailored to a specific situation.

The questions are grouped by subject. A reader in crisis can read only the category that fits. A reader who wants the full picture can read all five.

For the statute table, the preservation checklist, a glossary of terms, and reference material to bring to a first meeting with counsel, see the Appendix for Families that follows this one.

THE THREE CLOCKS

California trust and estate exploitation claims run on three separate statutes of limitation. They do not run together. A family that knows only one of them is often wrong about whether the case is over.

1. How long do I have to contest my father's trust in California?

In California, a beneficiary or heir typically has 120 days from the date the trustee serves a formal notice under Probate Code § 16061.7 to file a contest. The grounds include lack of capacity, undue influence, fraud, and the statutory presumption under Probate Code § 21380 that applies to transfers to drafters, caregivers, and fiduciaries. If the notice did not include a copy of the trust and you requested one, the period runs until the later of 120 days from the notice or 60 days from the date the trust is delivered. Chapter Five of this book describes what the notice looks like and why it is easy to miss.

2. What is the 120-day trust contest window?

The 120-day window is the period established by California Probate Code § 16061.7 within which a beneficiary or heir must file a petition contesting the validity of a trust after the trustee has served the statutorily required notice. The window applies to challenges based on capacity, undue influence, fraud, and the § 21380 presumption. After 120 days, those grounds are largely gone, though other claims—most notably financial elder abuse—may still be available under different statutes of limitation.

3. When does the 120-day clock actually start?

The clock starts on the date the trustee serves the notice required by Probate Code § 16061.7, not on the date of death and not on the date the family first learns the notice was sent.

Service is defined by the statute and typically means personal delivery or mail to the last known address. A notice that fails to meet the statutory content requirements—for example, one that omits the warning language required by § 16061.7(g)—does not start the clock at all. If you are uncertain whether the clock has started, have a California lawyer review the notice before assuming it has.

4. What if the trustee's notice did not include the trust document?

If the notice did not include the trust instrument, you have the right to request a copy, and the trustee must provide it. Once the trust is delivered, the contest window runs until the later of 120 days from the date of the original notice or 60 days from the date the trust is delivered. This rule exists to prevent a trustee from starting the clock on a recipient who has not yet seen what she is being asked to contest.

5. What if the notice was defective?

A notice that fails to meet the content requirements of California Probate Code § 16061.7 does not start the 120-day contest clock. Defects can include the wrong address, an incorrect or incomplete list of beneficiaries and heirs, or omission of the warning language the statute requires. Families who assume the window has closed are sometimes wrong about whether it ever opened. Before accepting that a case is over for timing reasons, have a California attorney examine the notice itself.

6. What is the four-year clock for financial elder abuse?

California Welfare and Institutions Code § 15657.7 establishes a four-year limitations period for financial elder abuse claims. The four years runs from the date the plaintiff discovered, or through reasonable diligence should have discovered, the facts giving rise to the claim—not from the date of the underlying transaction. Concealment by the wrongdoer can toll the period further. This is the statute that reaches drafting attorneys, caregivers, financial advisors, and other enablers described in Chapter Four.

7. When does the four-year clock start?

The four-year clock under California Welfare and Institutions Code § 15657.7 starts when the family learns, or reasonably should have learned, of the facts that suggest financial elder abuse—not when the document was signed and not when the elder died. For many families, discovery happens after the death, when they first read the trust and compare it to what their parent told them for years. If the other side concealed the abuse, the clock is tolled further.

8. What is the one-year clock for promise-to-inherit claims?

California Code of Civil Procedure § 366.3 establishes a one-year limitations period for claims arising from a promise to make a distribution at death. This applies, for example, to a child who stayed on a family farm for decades on the promise that the farm would come to her, only to find the trust said otherwise. The clock runs one year from the decedent's death. It is the narrowest and most easily missed of the three California clocks.

9. I missed the 120-day window. Is my case over?

Not necessarily. The 120-day trust contest window under California Probate Code § 16061.7 is only one of three clocks, and it closes first. The four-year financial elder abuse clock under Welfare and Institutions Code § 15657.7 often remains open, and it reaches not only the person who benefited but also the drafting attorney, the caregiver, and the financial advisor whose participation made the transaction possible. Before concluding the case is over, have a California trust litigation attorney review all three clocks against your specific facts. Chapter Five describes the elder abuse clock in detail.

Capacity and Undue Influence

California law does not ask what the doctor called the condition. It asks whether the person who signed understood what they were signing, and whether someone used that vulnerability to change the outcome.

10. Does my parent need to have had an Alzheimer's diagnosis to contest the trust?

No. California law does not require a specific diagnosis to establish lack of capacity or undue influence. The statutory standards under Probate Code §§ 810 through 813 ask whether the person understood the nature of the document, the people it affected, and the consequences of executing it—not what the underlying medical condition was called. Contests have succeeded on the basis of vascular dementia from silent stroke, alcohol-related cognitive decline, post-surgical confusion, and Lewy body dementia that was not diagnosed until autopsy. The diagnosis is not the point. The vulnerability is.

11. What is the legal standard for capacity to sign a trust in California?

California Probate Code §§ 810 through 813 establish the capacity standard. Capacity is presumed under § 810. The presumption can be rebutted by evidence of mental-function deficits—disorientation, impaired memory, impaired executive function, impaired ability to modulate mood—that correlate with the specific act in question. The standard asks whether, at the moment of signing, the person understood the nature of the document, the people it affected, and its consequences. Post-death reconstruction of capacity is done through medical records, forensic expert testimony, and the observations of percipient witnesses including the drafting attorney.

12. What is undue influence under California law?

California Welfare and Institutions Code § 15610.70 defines undue influence as excessive persuasion that causes another person to act or refrain from acting by overcoming that person's free will and resulting in inequity. The statute identifies four factors a court weighs: the victim's vulnerability, the influencer's apparent authority, the actions and tactics used, and the equity of the result. All four are relevant. None is dispositive on its own.

13. What is the § 21380 presumption?

California Probate Code § 21380 establishes a presumption that certain donative transfers are the product of undue influence and therefore invalid. The presumption applies to transfers to the person who drafted the instrument, to a care custodian who provided care in the 90 days before or any time after the execution, and to certain fiduciaries. When the presumption applies, the burden shifts: the recipient of the transfer must prove by clear and convincing evidence that the transfer was not the product of undue influence. Chapter Four of this book describes how this framework reaches drafting attorneys and caregivers.

14. Who counts as a "care custodian" under § 21380?

Under California Probate Code § 21380, a care custodian is a person who provides health or social services to a dependent adult. The California Supreme Court's decision in Bernard v. Foley established that care-custodian status is determined by function, not by job title—a caregiver who was never formally employed as one can still qualify. A transfer from a dependent adult to a care custodian is presumptively invalid, with a narrow exception under § 21382 for blood relatives within the fourth degree.

15. What is a Certificate of Independent Review?

A Certificate of Independent Review, under California Probate Code § 21384, is a written certification by an independent attorney—one who has no connection to the transferee—that a donative transfer subject to the § 21380 presumption was not the product of fraud or undue influence. A properly executed Certificate rebuts the presumption. Many transfers that might otherwise be invalid stand because a Certificate was obtained. Many that should have been obtained were not. Whether a Certificate exists—and whether the attorney who signed it was genuinely independent—is an early question in any California § 21380 case.

16. Does the presumption apply if the caregiver is a family member?

California Probate Code § 21382 provides a narrow exception for transfers to the transferor's spouse and to blood relatives within the fourth degree. A biological child who cared for a parent and then received a transfer is not subject to the § 21380 presumption on that basis. This does not mean the transfer is unchallengeable—undue influence and capacity claims remain available under the general framework of Welfare and Institutions Code § 15610.70 and Probate Code §§ 810 through 813. It means the burden-shifting mechanism of § 21380 does not apply.

17. How do you prove capacity or lack of capacity after the person has died?

Post-death capacity analysis in California is reconstructed from four sources: contemporaneous medical records covering the period before and after the signing, the observations of the drafting attorney and other percipient witnesses, the surrounding documentary record including texts and emails, and the opinions of forensic experts—typically neurologists, forensic psychiatrists, or neuropsychologists—who apply the Probate Code § 811 criteria to the record. The drafting attorney's file, which becomes available under Evidence Code §§ 957 and 961 after the client's death, is often the most important single piece of evidence. Chapter Four describes why.

WHEN PROFESSIONALS MADE IT POSSIBLE

A California elder financial abuse claim reaches every person whose participation made the wrongful transaction possible—not only the person who benefited. Drafting attorneys, financial advisors, accountants, and notaries are not peripheral figures. They are the infrastructure. This category describes the framework Chapter Four of this book lays out in full.

18. Can the attorney who drafted the trust be sued?

Yes. Under California Welfare and Institutions Code § 15657.7 and the related framework for financial elder abuse, a drafting attorney whose participation made a wrongful transaction possible can be named as a defendant. Liability attaches where the attorney knew or reasonably should have known that the client lacked capacity or was being subjected to undue influence, and drafted the document anyway. Mandatory attorney's fees on recovery under § 15657.5 apply. Double damages on a finding of bad faith apply under Probate Code § 859.

19. Can the drafting attorney be deposed?

Yes. The drafting attorney is a percipient witness to the execution of the document and to the client's condition at the time of signing. California Evidence Code § 957 provides a testamentary exception to the attorney-client privilege: in a dispute between parties claiming through a deceased client, communications relevant to the dispute are discoverable. Evidence Code § 961 reaches communications relevant to the deceased client's intentions concerning a written instrument affecting property. In practical terms, the attorney's file and the attorney's testimony about the signing are both routinely available in a California trust contest.

20. Is the attorney-client privilege a defense to deposition?

Not fully. The attorney-client privilege belongs to the client, not to the lawyer, and the lawyer's own observations of the client's capacity and conduct at the signing are not privileged communications—they are the lawyer's own perceptions as a witness. California Evidence Code §§ 957 and 961 further permit discovery of communications themselves in disputes between parties claiming through a deceased client. The privilege exists to protect the client; once the client is gone and the dispute is about what the client intended, the file typically becomes the clearest evidence of the client's mental state at the moment of signing.

21. Can the drafting attorney be disqualified from defending the trust?

Yes, and the motion is often granted. A drafting attorney who is a material witness to the execution of the instrument cannot ordinarily both testify and serve as advocate in the same litigation. The California Rules of Professional Conduct, particularly Rules 1.7 and 1.9, govern conflicts that arise from the drafter's dual role as witness and advocate. The California Supreme Court addressed the underlying principles in Flatt v. Superior Court. Disqualification is a motion filed early in the case and, when successful, removes the person most invested in defending the signing from the defense team.

22. Can the trust pay the defense lawyers?

Not where the trustee's conduct is alleged to breach fiduciary duty. California Probate Code § 15684 limits a trustee's right to reimbursement from trust assets to expenses properly incurred in the administration of the trust. A trustee accused of misappropriation cannot use the contested assets to fund a defense against the beneficiary alleging the misappropriation. The California decisions in Pizarro v. Reynoso and Kasperbauer v. Fairfield develop this principle. A family that discovers the defense is being funded from the trust has, in California, an additional claim and an additional basis for recovery.

23. What happens if the trust has already been paying the defense lawyers?

Trust funds paid to defense counsel while the trustee's conduct is contested can be recovered through a California Probate Code § 850 petition, which authorizes recovery of trust property from any third party holding it. A defense attorney who has been formally notified that the fees are unauthorized and continues to accept them has, by the law's definition, actual knowledge. Under Probate Code § 859, damages are doubled on a finding of bad faith. The consequence is personal liability for the defense attorney, not only for the client.

24. Can the financial advisor be sued for moving money at someone else's direction?

Yes. A California financial elder abuse claim under Welfare and Institutions Code § 15657.7 reaches any person whose participation facilitated the wrongful transaction, including registered investment advisors, brokers, and financial planners who executed transfers at the direction of a person who was not the account holder. Advisors who observed signs of cognitive decline in their client and continued to follow the direction of a family member, caregiver, or new spouse face potential liability.

Account freezes, preservation letters, and production of advisor files are standard first steps.

25. Can the accountant or notary who witnessed the signing be liable?

Potentially, yes. California financial elder abuse liability under Welfare and Institutions Code § 15657.7 extends to any participant whose conduct made the wrongful transaction possible. An accountant who facilitated the execution of a document she knew would strip a family of its inheritance, or a notary who completed a signing she observed to be irregular, can be named as a defendant. The analysis turns on what the professional knew or reasonably should have known at the time. Chapter Four of this book describes how these claims are developed.

The First Thirty Days

What a California family does in the first month after discovery shapes what any lawyer can do in the months after. The moves below are the ones that matter most.

26. What should I do right now if I think my parent was exploited?

Four things, in priority order. Preserve everything—emails, texts, voicemails, photographs, documents, and anything else from the months before and after the signing. Write down what you remember, dated. Do not confront the other party. Do not sign any settlement, waiver, or release that arrives without a California attorney reviewing it first. These four moves can be made in the first week and they do not require a lawyer to be in place. Chapter Six describes each in detail.

27. Should I call the trustee and confront them?

No. A call in the first week gives the other side a preview of your case, eliminates the element of surprise a preservation letter would otherwise provide, and often produces recorded statements the family later wishes it had not made. The conversation that needs to happen will happen, under your attorney's direction, with preservation obligations already in place. Wait.

28. Should I sign what they are asking me to sign?

Not without independent California legal review. Settlement offers, waivers, receipts, and releases sometimes arrive in the first weeks after a death. A signature in week two can foreclose a recovery in month three. Anything asking for a signature —from the trustee, from counsel for the estate, or from a financial institution—should be set aside until a California trust litigation attorney of your choosing has reviewed it.

29. What is a preservation letter and what does it do?

A preservation letter is a written notice from your attorney requiring the recipient to retain records and electronic evidence that may be relevant to potential litigation. In California, it is sent to the trustee, to the drafting attorney, to financial institutions holding trust assets, and to any other party whose records are likely to matter. It creates a legal duty to preserve and triggers spoliation consequences under California Code of Civil Procedure § 2023.030 and cases including Cedars-Sinai Medical Center v. Superior Court if records are subsequently destroyed. It is often the first act of legal leverage in a case, sent within days of the initial meeting.

30. What is lis pendens and when should it be filed?

A lis pendens, governed by California Code of Civil Procedure §§ 405 through 405.61, is a recorded notice that a lawsuit involving real property is pending. Once recorded, a buyer cannot purchase the property free of the claim. In estate exploitation cases involving a house or other real property, a lis pendens is filed to prevent an arm's-length sale that would otherwise put the property beyond the reach of the family's claim. The timing is important—lis pendens is most effective when recorded early, before the property is marketed.

31. What evidence should I preserve?

Everything, without editing. Emails, text messages, voicemails, letters, photographs, recordings, calendar entries, financial statements, and medical records. Screenshots of text threads with visible dates. Copies of documents the parent received or signed. Forward important emails to a dedicated address so later deletion does not eliminate the record. Do not delete anything from the months preceding or following the signing. The item that looks trivial now may be central at deposition.

32. When should I call a lawyer?

As soon as you recognize the pattern. California trust contest windows can close in as little as 120 days from the trustee's notice. Evidence decays, witnesses scatter, and assets dissipate in the months after a death. The first meeting with a California trust litigation attorney can often be scheduled within days of the initial call and is used to identify which clocks are running, which theories are available, and what preservation steps need to happen immediately. The honest advice of a lawyer who has done this work is more valuable than the confident advice of one who has not.

33. What should I bring to the first meeting with a lawyer?

The § 16061.7 notice, if you have received one. The trust and any amendments. The will. The death certificate. Dated notes from the period before the death. Preserved evidence, organized by date. A list of known and unknown assets. A list of the people who were present in your parent's life in the last year—family, caregivers, neighbors, visitors, and professionals. Chapter Six and the Appendix for Families list the full preparation checklist.

The Economics of Litigation

California trust and elder abuse litigation is among the most expensive areas of civil law. The economics determine which cases can be pursued and how. These questions are the ones families ask in the first call.

34. How much does a California trust contest cost?

A moderately complex California trust contest—single settlor, two beneficiaries, allegations of undue influence, one expert on capacity—typically costs between 75,000 and 150,000 dollars per side through the point of mediation or early settlement. A case that proceeds to a full trial can cost 200,000 to 300,000 dollars per side. These are not unusual numbers. They are the ordinary cost of this kind of litigation and they are the reason most California trust and elder abuse matters are handled on contingency rather than hourly.

35. What is a contingency fee arrangement?

Under a contingency fee agreement, the attorney is paid a percentage of the recovery, and the client pays no hourly fee. If there is no recovery, the attorney is not paid. California contingency fee agreements are governed by Business and Professions Code § 6147, which requires that they be in writing, signed by both client and attorney, and include specified disclosures. Contingency is the arrangement that makes California trust and elder abuse litigation accessible to families who could not otherwise afford to litigate. Chapter Eleven of this book describes how this economic reality shapes which cases are pursued.

36. Can I recover attorney's fees if I win?

In California financial elder abuse cases, yes—and the fees are mandatory on recovery, not discretionary. Welfare and Institutions Code § 15657.5 requires the court to award reasonable attorney's fees and costs to a plaintiff who establishes elder financial abuse. This is a significant feature of California law. The people who took the money pay the fees of the lawyer the family hired to get it back. The fee-shifting provision is part of why the elder abuse framework reaches further than a traditional trust contest.

37. Are damages doubled in elder financial abuse cases?

In California, damages may be doubled in certain cases. Probate Code § 859 authorizes double damages on a finding that the wrongful taking of property was done in bad faith. This applies to property recovered through § 850 petitions and reaches any person—not only trustees—who wrongfully took, concealed, or disposed of property belonging to an estate or trust. Combined with mandatory attorney's fees under Welfare and Institutions Code § 15657.5, the doubled damages reshape the economic calculation both before litigation and during settlement negotiations.

38. What if the estate is small?

Small-estate cases are harder to bring on contingency because the expected recovery must substantially exceed the cost of litigation. California attorneys handling elder financial abuse cases on contingency must match their intake to cases where the economics work—where the estate is reachable, the assets identifiable, and the recovery sufficient to justify the investment. Chapter 11 of this book addresses this directly. Many families with legitimate cases are unable to find contingency representation. For those families, understanding the law is often the most practical help available, which is one reason this book exists.

CYBER EXPLOITATION AND THE SCREEN

An increasing share of elder financial exploitation now arrives through the screen rather than through the front door. The money is typically not recoverable, but understanding what happened is often the first step toward preventing the next act of exploitation.

39. My parent was scammed online. Can the money be recovered?

Usually, no. Funds lost to cyber-enabled fraud—romance scams, tech-support scams, pig-butchering cryptocurrency schemes—move through chains of accounts in foreign jurisdictions that do not cooperate with U.S. recovery efforts, and are typically converted to assets or physical currency beyond the reach of U.S. civil process. Reporting the fraud to the FBI's Internet Crime Complaint Center at ic3.gov and to local law enforcement is the correct first step. Preventing further transfers is usually more achievable than recovering what was sent. Chapter Seven describes these cases.

40. What is pig-butchering?

Pig-butchering is a translation of the Mandarin sha zhu pan, used by the organized criminal enterprises that run the scheme. A victim is contacted on a messaging application, a dating platform, or a social network. Over weeks of cultivated conversation, the victim is introduced to a fraudulent cryptocurrency or investment platform that displays fabricated balances and small withdrawals that succeed. The victim invests progressively larger sums. When the victim attempts a large withdrawal, the platform demands "tax" or "clearance" fees that are themselves additional theft. The funds are long gone by the time the fraud is discovered.

41. Who should I report an online elder scam to?

Three authorities, in combination. The FBI's Internet Crime Complaint Center at ic3.gov is the primary federal channel for cyber-enabled financial fraud. Local law enforcement should receive a report because some investigative coordination happens at the state and county level. The Federal Trade Commission at reportfraud.ftc.gov handles identity theft and imposter scams. For California residents, Adult Protective Services in the relevant county is an additional channel, and in some cases a preferred one, because elder-specific resources and follow-up may be available.

42. Can we sue the bank or wire service that processed the transfers?

Sometimes, under narrow circumstances. California law imposes certain fiduciary duties on financial institutions with respect to elder clients, and the Electronic Fund Transfer Act under 15 U.S.C. § 1693 and Regulation E provide limited protections in a small subset of cases. Most cyber-scam wires are authorized by the victim, which places them outside EFTA protection. Liability for the institution is most often pursued where the institution ignored documented red flags—such as a senior client wiring large sums to unfamiliar foreign accounts—or where a registered investment advisor breached fiduciary duties to a vulnerable client. These cases are fact-specific and require early consultation with counsel experienced in financial institution liability.

The answers in this appendix are starting points. None of them replaces advice from a California attorney who has reviewed the specific facts of a specific case. What they do is give a family the vocabulary to have the right conversation—with a lawyer, with a sibling, with a parent who may still be well enough to act. That vocabulary is often the difference between a recovery and a case that never gets filed.

Knowledge is not justice. But it is the next best thing.

Appendix: For Families

This appendix is organized as reference material. It does not replace a lawyer. It gives the reader the vocabulary and the framework to have the right conversation—with a lawyer, with a family member, with a parent who may still be healthy enough to act.

For direct answers to common legal questions—what the 120-day clock is, whether a drafting attorney can be sued, how much a case costs—see the Questions and Answers Appendix.

The Three Clocks

Every California estate dispute runs on clocks. A family that does not know which clock governs—or that there are three—loses options it did not know it had.

The 120-Day Clock—Probate Code § 16061.7

The trustee of a trust that has become irrevocable at the settlor's death must serve formal notice on beneficiaries and certain heirs within sixty days. Once served, the recipient has one hundred and twenty days to file a contest. Grounds include lack of capacity, undue influence, fraud, and the § 21380 presumption that applies to transfers to drafters, caregivers, and fiduciaries. After one hundred and twenty days, those grounds are largely gone.

If the notice does not include the trust document, the recipient may request a copy. The trustee must provide it. The contest period runs until the later of one hundred and twenty days from service of the notice or sixty days from the date the trust is delivered.

A defective notice—wrong address, missing the statutorily required warning language, served on the wrong person—does not start the clock. A family that believes the window has closed should have a lawyer review the notice before accepting that conclusion.

The Four-Year Clock—Welfare and Institutions Code § 15657.7

Financial elder abuse claims run four years from discovery, not from the transaction. The clock is delayed-discovery tolled: it begins when the family learns the facts that would suggest abuse, not when the document was signed. Concealment tolls the clock further.

This is the primary claim in most of the cases in this book. It reaches not only the person who benefited but also the professionals whose participation made the transaction possible —drafting attorneys, caregivers, financial advisors, accountants. Under Welfare and Institutions Code § 15657.5, attorney's fees are mandatory on recovery. Under Probate Code § 859, damages are doubled on a finding of bad faith.

The One-Year Clock—Code of Civil Procedure § 366.3

A narrow clock. It applies to claims arising from a promise

to make a distribution at death—a parent who promised a child, for decades, that the farm would come to her if she stayed, and then signed a trust saying otherwise. One year from the decedent's death. It is the shortest and the most easily missed. It runs from death, not from notice and not from discovery.

Key California Statutes

The statutes below appear throughout the book. This table gives each a short plain-English description.

Citation	**What it does**
Welf. & Inst. Code § 15610.30	Defines financial elder abuse
Welf. & Inst. Code § 15610.70	Four-factor test for undue influence
Welf. & Inst. Code § 15657.5	Mandatory attorney's fees on elder abuse recovery
Welf. & Inst. Code § 15657.7	Four-year limitations period on financial elder abuse
Prob. Code § 810 to § 813	Standards for capacity
Prob. Code § 16061.7	120-day trust contest window after formal notice
Prob. Code § 17200	Petitions concerning trust administration (removal, accounting, instructions)
Prob. Code § 21380	Presumptively invalid donative transfers to drafters, caregivers, fiduciaries
Prob. Code § 850	Recovery of property wrongfully transferred
Prob. Code § 859	Double damages on finding of bad faith

| Code Civ. Proc. § 366.3 | One-year limitations period on promise-to-inherit claims |

| Evid. Code § 957 | Testamentary exception to attorney-client privilege |

THE FIRST THIRTY DAYS

The preservation moves a family can make in the first month—preserve everything, dated notes, do not confront, do not sign—are answered in depth in the Questions and Answers appendix at Questions 26 through 33. That material is not repeated here. **See Questions 26 through 33.**

RED FLAGS—BEFORE THE DEATH

The patterns in this book are identifiable while the elder is still alive. A family that recognizes them early has tools the post-death family does not.

A new person in the house—a caregiver, a neighbor, a new spouse, a long-estranged child who has returned. Physical isolation—locks changed, phone calls screened, visits discouraged or denied. Sudden change in estate-planning professionals—new attorney, new financial advisor, new accountant, particularly ones the new person introduced. A parent's communication pattern that has changed—calls only at certain times, calls not returned, voice or tone different during calls. Credit card activity the parent would not have made. Large cash withdrawals. Wire transfers to unfamiliar recipients. A parent who repeats things, forgets recent events, becomes disoriented—and no one has obtained a capacity evaluation. A parent who tells the family the estate plan has not changed.

Verify.

Red Flags—In the Document

A trust or amendment is not automatically valid because it was notarized. The patterns below, drawn from the cases in this book, are commonly seen in documents that do not hold up.

Executed during a hospitalization or within days of one. Executed within days of a surgery, a rehab discharge, or an acute medical event. Executed by a parent who cannot drive themselves to the attorney's office. Executed without independent counsel, where a family member or caregiver selected the drafter. Children's names misspelled. Addresses wrong. Relationships described incorrectly. A complete restatement signed on the same day as multiple other documents. A beneficiary newly added who had known the parent for less than a year. A caregiver named as beneficiary, trustee, or both.

Meeting with Counsel

What to bring to the first meeting, what counsel will ask, and what counsel should tell you are covered in the Questions and Answers appendix. **See Questions 32 and 33.**

A lawyer who promises a quick result has not read the file. A lawyer who guarantees recovery on the first call should be treated with the skepticism the guarantee warrants.

Glossary

Beneficiary. A person entitled to receive property or benefits from a trust or estate.

Capacity. The legal standard for whether a person understood the nature of what they were signing at the moment they signed. Governed by Probate Code §§ 810 through 813.

Care custodian. Under Probate Code § 21380, a person who provides health or social services to a dependent adult. Transfers from a dependent adult to a care custodian are presumptively invalid, with a narrow exception for blood relatives.

Certificate of Independent Review. A written certification by an independent attorney, under Probate Code § 21384, that a donative transfer subject to the § 21380 presumption was not the product of undue influence. Rebuts the presumption when properly executed.

Conservator. A person appointed by a court to manage the affairs of an incapacitated adult. Conservatorship is usually a last resort; alternatives include power of attorney and trust-based management.

Contest. A challenge to the validity of a will or trust. Trust contests must ordinarily be filed within the one-hundred-twenty-day window of Probate Code § 16061.7.

Delayed discovery. The rule under which a statute of limitations does not begin to run until the plaintiff knew or reasonably should have known of the facts giving rise to the claim. Applies to financial elder abuse claims under Welfare and Institutions Code § 15657.7.

Fiduciary duty. The legal obligation of a trustee, agent, attorney-in-fact, or similar figure to act in the best interests of the person they serve.

HEMS. Health, education, maintenance, and support—the common standard governing trustee discretion over distributions to a beneficiary.

Heir. A person entitled to receive property under intestacy law when the decedent left no valid will or trust.

Incapacity. The functional absence of capacity. Different legal standards apply for different acts—testamentary capacity, contractual capacity, capacity to marry.

Intestate. Dying without a valid will or trust. The estate passes under California's statutory succession rules.

Irrevocable trust. A trust that cannot be amended or revoked by the settlor after execution, with narrow exceptions. Most trusts become irrevocable at the settlor's death.

Lis pendens. A recorded notice that a lawsuit is pending involving real property. Prevents arm's-length sales to third parties who would otherwise take title free of the claim.

Marital trust. A trust established for the benefit of a surviving spouse, often with remainder to the decedent's children from a prior marriage. See Chapter Eight.

Notice (under § 16061.7). The formal notification sent by a trustee to beneficiaries and heirs after a trust becomes irrevocable at death. Starts the one-hundred-twenty-day contest clock.

Percipient witness. A witness who observed the events at issue. A drafting attorney who observed the signing is a percipient witness to the client's capacity and conduct, and cannot claim privilege over those observations.

Power of attorney. A document authorizing one person to act on behalf of another. Durable powers survive the principal's incapacity.

Preservation letter. A written notice sent by a family or their counsel requiring the recipient to preserve documents and electronic records for potential litigation. Triggers spoliation consequences if records are later destroyed.

Probate. The court-supervised process of administering a decedent's estate. Trust administration is usually non-probate.

Remainder beneficiary. A person entitled to receive the assets of a trust after the current beneficiary's interest ends—typically, the children of a first marriage who receive what remains of a marital trust after the surviving spouse's death.

Restatement. A comprehensive rewriting of an existing trust, replacing the prior instrument while keeping the same trust's identity.

Settlor. The person who creates a trust. Also called the grantor or trustor.

Successor trustee. The person designated to serve as trustee after the initial trustee dies, resigns, or is removed.

Testamentary capacity. The capacity required to make a valid will. Generally a lower standard than contractual capacity.

Trust. A legal arrangement in which one person (the trustee) holds property for the benefit of another (the beneficiary).

Trustee. The person who manages the trust. Owes fiduciary duties to the beneficiaries.

Undue influence. The use of excessive persuasion—through vulnerability, apparent authority, tactics, and inequitable result—to cause a person to execute a document they would not otherwise have executed. Defined in Welfare and Institutions Code § 15610.70.

Resources

AARP. aarp.org. Consumer protection and elder financial exploitation resources, including the AARP Fraud Watch Network helpline for suspected scams and financial abuse.

California Department of Aging—Adult Protective Services (APS). aging.ca.gov. Every California county maintains an Adult Protective Services office that receives reports of suspected elder abuse. Reports can be made by family members, neighbors, or the elder. Identity of the reporter is kept confidential by statute.

California Courts Self-Help Center. selfhelp.courts.ca.gov. Plain-language guidance on probate and trust matters, including forms for pro se litigants.

State Bar of California Lawyer Referral Service. calbar.ca.gov. Referrals to California attorneys by practice area, including trust and estate litigation.

Legal Services Corporation. lsc.gov. Federal funding source for civil legal aid. Directory of local legal aid organizations for low-income families who may qualify for free representation.

Federal Bureau of Investigation—Internet Crime Complaint Center (IC3). ic3.gov. For online fraud, tech support scams, romance scams, cryptocurrency investment fraud, and related cybercrime. Reports are routed to appropriate federal and local agencies.

Federal Trade Commission. reportfraud.ftc.gov. For identity theft, imposter scams, and consumer fraud affecting older adults.

National Center on Elder Abuse. ncea.acl.gov. Federal resource center on elder abuse prevention, research, and state-by-state reporting information.

Notes On Sources

The cases in this book, with the exceptions identified in the Author's Note, are anonymized composites drawn from five decades of California trust and estate litigation. The legal framework is not. What follows identifies the statutes, rules, and doctrines underlying the substantive claims made in each chapter.

Introduction

The framing that California law asks whether the signer understood what they were signing—rather than what the doctor called the underlying condition—reflects the capacity standards in Probate Code §§ 810 through 813. Section 810 establishes the presumption of capacity. Section 811 enumerates the mental-function deficits that can rebut that presumption and requires a correlation between deficit and specific act. Section 812 defines the general capacity standard for making decisions.

Section 813 sets a lower threshold for capacity to make medical decisions.

The one-hundred-twenty-day reference comes from Probate Code § 16061.7 and the associated contest-period rules in § 16061.8.

Chapter One: When It Isn't Alzheimer's

The principle that undue influence analysis does not require a specific diagnosis is rooted in Welfare and Institutions Code § 15610.70, which defines undue influence through four factors: vulnerability of the victim, influencer's apparent authority, actions and tactics used, and equity of the result.

The § 21380 presumption invalidating donative transfers to drafters, care custodians, and fiduciaries is discussed in detail in Chapter Four and the Notes there.

The legal standard—whether the person understood the nature of the document, the people it affected, and the consequences of executing it—is drawn from Probate Code § 812 and the capacity criteria in § 811. Post-hoc reconstruction of capacity at the moment of signing is a standard practice in trust contests; the methodology relies on contemporaneous medical records, the deficit-correlation requirement of § 811, and expert testimony by neurologists, forensic psychiatrists, and neuropsychologists.

Chapter Two: When the Stranger Moves In

The four questions the law asks—vulnerability, apparent authority, tactics, and equity of result—are the statutory factors under Welfare and Institutions Code § 15610.70. These apply identically whether the influencer is a stranger, a caretaker, or a biological child.

The enhanced remedies for transfers procured by undue influence include the § 21380 presumption of invalidity (discussed in Chapter Four), recovery of property under Probate Code § 850, and mandatory attorney's fees on a finding of financial elder abuse under Welfare and Institutions Code § 15657.5.

Chapter Three: The People Who Made It Possible

The percipient-witness doctrine as applied to drafting attorneys reflects long-settled California evidence law. The attorney-client privilege belongs to the client, not the lawyer; the lawyer's own observations of the client's capacity and conduct are not privileged communications.

The post-death exception allowing parties to obtain attorney-client communications in estate disputes is governed by Evidence Code § 957 (communications relevant to issues between parties claiming through the deceased client) and § 961 (communications relevant to deceased client's intention concerning a written document affecting an interest in property). In combination, these sections make the drafting attorney's file routinely discoverable in a will or trust contest.

Disqualification of the drafting attorney from defending the instrument he created derives from California Rule of Professional Conduct 1.7 (conflicts of interest—current clients), Rule 1.9 (duties to former clients), and the California Supreme Court's decision in *Flatt v. Superior Court*, 9 Cal.4th 275 (1994). The lawyer cannot simultaneously defend the drafting process and serve as advocate for a party adverse to other parties with whom he has had a confidential attorney-client relationship.

The § 21380 presumption—that donative transfers to the drafter of the instrument, to the transferor's care custodian, or to certain fiduciaries are presumed to be the product of undue influence—is codified in Probate Code § 21380. Exceptions are set forth in § 21382 (most notably for blood relatives within the fourth degree) and § 21384 (Certificate of Independent Review). The Supreme Court's decision in *Bernard v. Foley*, 39 Cal.4th 794 (2006), established that care-custodian status is determined by function, not title.

The rule limiting trustee indemnification from trust assets for legal expenses is drawn from Probate Code § 15684 (reimbursement of trustee expenses), § 15642 (grounds for removal), and the California Supreme Court's decision in *Pizarro v. Reynoso*, 10 Cal.App.5th 172 (2017). The related rule prohibiting a trustee accused of misappropriation from funding his defense out of the contested assets is developed in *Kasperbauer v. Fairfield*, 171 Cal.App.4th 229 (2009).

Recovery of trust property held by third parties—including legal fees paid to defense counsel from contested trust funds—is authorized by Probate Code § 850. Double damages on a finding of bad faith are provided under Probate Code § 859. Mandatory attorney's fees on an elder financial abuse recovery are provided under Welfare and Institutions Code § 15657.5.

CHAPTER FOUR: THE ENVELOPE THAT LOOKED LIKE NOTHING

The one-hundred-twenty-day trust contest clock derives from Probate Code § 16061.7 (notification requirement) and § 16061.8 (contest period). The contest period runs one hundred and twenty days from service of the notice or sixty days from the date the trust is delivered in response to a proper request, whichever is later.

The defective-notice doctrine—that a notice failing to meet the content requirements of § 16061.7(g) does not start the clock—is established by the statutory language and developed in *Harustak v. Wilkins*, 84 Cal.App.4th 208 (2000).

The four-year limitations period on financial elder abuse claims is Welfare and Institutions Code § 15657.7, which measures the period from the date the plaintiff discovered or, through the exercise of reasonable diligence, should have discovered the facts constituting the abuse. This is a delayed-discovery rule, and concealment by the wrongdoer can toll the period further.

The one-year limitations period for claims arising from a promise to make a distribution on death is Code of Civil Procedure § 366.3. See *Stewart v. Seward*, 148 Cal.App.4th 1513 (2007), which applied § 366.3 to a promise-based inheritance claim.

The three clocks run independently and address different theories of liability; none is a substitute for the others.

Chapter Five: The First Thirty Days

The statutory framework identified in the chapter—§ 16061.7, § 15657.7, and § 366.3—is sourced as in the Chapter Five notes.

The preservation-letter practice and the doctrine of spoliation of evidence derive from multiple authorities, including Code of Civil Procedure § 2023.030 (discovery sanctions, including evidentiary sanctions for spoliation), *Cedars-Sinai Medical Center v. Superior Court*, 18 Cal.4th 1 (1998), and *Williams v. Russ*, 167 Cal.App.4th 1215 (2008). The heightened duty of trustees to preserve records is reinforced by the trustee's general duty of disclosure under Probate Code §§ 16060 through 16062.

The lis pendens authority referenced in the tools section derives from Code of Civil Procedure §§ 405 through 405.61.

The temporary trustee and trustee suspension remedies are authorized under Probate Code § 17200 (scope of trust petitions) and § 15642 (grounds for removal and suspension).

Contingency fee agreements in California are governed by Business and Professions Code § 6147.

Chapter Six: Through the Screen

The reporting resources identified in the chapter—the FBI's Internet Crime Complaint Center (ic3.gov) and local law enforcement—are the primary federal and state channels for cybercrime and elder-targeted financial fraud reports. Related federal authorities include 18 U.S.C. § 1343 (wire fraud) and 18 U.S.C. § 1030 (computer fraud and abuse).

Electronic Fund Transfer Act protections under 15 U.S.C. § 1693 et seq. and Regulation E (12 C.F.R. Part 1005) apply in a limited subset of these cases. Most pig-butchering and romance scams fall outside those protections because the victim authorizes the transfer.

"Pig-butchering" is a translation of the Mandarin 杀猪盘 (*sha zhu pan*), a term used by the criminal enterprises that run the schemes. Federal and state prosecutors have begun using the term in charging documents and public guidance.

The fiduciary duty of registered investment advisors is established under the Investment Advisers Act of 1940, 15 U.S.C. § 80b-6, and developed in the SEC's Commission Interpretation Regarding Standard of Conduct for Investment Advisers, Release No. IA-5248 (June 5, 2019). FINRA Rule 2165 authorizes member firms to place temporary holds on disbursements from accounts of specified adults where financial exploitation is reasonably suspected. FINRA Rule 4512 requires firms to obtain the name and contact information of a trusted contact person for each senior customer account. Regulation Best Interest is codified at 17 C.F.R. § 240.15l-1. The federal Senior Safe Act is at Public Law 115-174, § 303 (2018), and provides immunity from suit to financial institutions that report suspected exploitation in good faith.

California elder financial abuse liability for financial institutions turns on Welfare and Institutions Code §§ 15610.23 (dependent adult), 15610.27 (elder), and 15610.30 (financial abuse, including conduct that assists in the wrongful taking of property). Mandatory attorney's fees on recovery are provided under § 15657.5, and double damages on a finding of bad faith are provided under Probate Code § 859, as cited elsewhere in these Notes.

CHAPTER SEVEN: THE STRUCTURE THAT STARTS THE WAR

The account of Richard Blum's and Dianne Feinstein's estate dispute is drawn from the public court filings in *In the matter of The Richard C. Blum & Dianne Feinstein Joint Property Revocable Trust*, San Francisco Superior Court, filed June 27, 2023; the subsequent actions filed by Katherine Feinstein over the following two months; and contemporaneous reporting in the *San Francisco Chronicle*, NBC News, and the Associated Press. The specific trust terms—including the five-million-dollar funding requirement for the marital trust and the minimum one-and-a-half-million-dollar annual distribution—are as described in the public complaint.

The Berkeley hotel sale figure of approximately one hundred and sixty-three million dollars was reported in the third-lawsuit filings and in SFGATE's and the San Francisco Chronicle's coverage.

Dianne Feinstein died on September 29, 2023.

The financial elder abuse claim under Welfare and Institutions Code § 15657.7, incorporating the definition in Welfare and Institutions Code § 15610.30, was the basis of the third-filed action.

The marital-trust structure more generally is a standard estate-planning device designed to qualify for the federal estate tax marital deduction under Internal Revenue Code § 2056(b)(7) (qualified terminable interest property, or QTIP, trusts) while preserving the remainder for the deceased spouse's children. The fiduciary tensions described in the chapter are inherent in the structure.

The account of Robin Williams's and Susan Schneider's estate dispute is drawn from the public court filings in San Francisco Superior Court beginning December 2014, and from contemporaneous reporting and subsequent commentary in the estate-planning literature. The trust provisions, including the specific language at issue ("memorabilia," "jewelry," "all costs related to the residence"), are as described in the widow's petition.

The diagnosis of diffuse Lewy body dementia was confirmed by autopsy and reported by the Lewy Body Dementia Association and in subsequent peer-reviewed literature on the clinical features of the disease. Lewy body dementia is characterized by cognitive fluctuation, recurrent visual hallucinations, REM sleep behavior disorder, and parkinsonism.

Unlike Alzheimer's disease, which principally affects memory in its early stages, Lewy body dementia commonly affects judgment, attention, and executive function earlier in its course.

The reader interested in the clinical profile should consult the diagnostic criteria of the DLB Consortium as most recently updated.

Chapter Eight: What the Record Remembers

The capacity framework applied throughout the chapter derives from Probate Code §§ 810 through 813. The question the chapter turns on—whether the decedent understood what she was signing at the moment of signing—is the § 812 standard, assessed through the deficit-correlation requirements of § 811.

The evidentiary use of records not prepared in anticipation of litigation—text messages, voicemails, unmailed correspondence, and similar materials—reflects the ordinary application of California evidence law. Such records are typically admitted under Evidence Code §§ 1250 (then-existing state of mind) and 1410 (authentication by distinctive characteristics, including handwriting), subject to the hearsay framework of Evidence Code §§ 1200 and following. Forensic document examination and forensic neuropsychological analysis of recorded speech are established evidentiary methods in California trust-contest practice.

The testamentary exception to the attorney-client privilege —referenced in the Eleanor section—is codified at Evidence Code § 957 (communications relevant to issues between parties claiming through a deceased client) and § 961 (communications relevant to the deceased client's intentions concerning a written instrument affecting an interest in property). The drafting attorney's file becomes discoverable on the client's death in a dispute over what the client intended.

Rapidly progressive vascular dementia following a silent cerebrovascular event is a recognized clinical entity in the geriatric literature. The clinical and neuroradiological features are described in the standard reference works, including the diagnostic criteria of the Vascular Impairment of Cognition Classification Consensus Study. Post-mortem confirmation of a vascular etiology for progressive cognitive decline is routine in cases where no diagnosis was made during life.

The principle that records outlast silence is an observation drawn from fifty years of California trust and estate litigation practice, not a legal doctrine. The statutory and evidentiary frameworks the chapter illustrates apply across California and, with state-specific variations, across the United States.

CHAPTER NINE: THE WINDOW

The trust revocation mechanics described—that a settlor's right to revoke under the express terms of a trust instrument typically operates independently of the trustee-succession-on-incapacity provisions—reflect the general rule that trust terms govern, subject to Probate Code §§ 15400 through 15414 (revocation and modification).

The § 21380 family-member exception referenced in the discussion of Frances and Daniel is codified at Probate Code § 21382(a), which excepts from the § 21380 presumption transfers to the transferor's spouse and to blood relatives within the fourth degree. The exception applies without regard to the recipient's occupation or conflicts of interest.

The observation that the law recognizes two states of mind —capacity and incapacity—is a simplification. Probate Code §§

810 through 813 describe capacity as a continuum, with different standards for different acts and different mental-function deficits. The simplification serves the narrative.

Chapter Ten: How Cases End: Three Mediations

The non-enforcement of the HEMS standard (health, education, maintenance, and support) described in the second mediation story derives from the general rule that trust modification is disfavored where it would defeat the settlor's intent. See Probate Code § 15403 (modification by consent of settlor and beneficiaries) and § 15409 (modification by court order due to changed circumstances). The structural solution described—using the trust's own mediation and trustee-appointment provisions rather than seeking court modification—is consistent with the settlor-intent principle.

The California witness requirements for wills are set forth in Probate Code § 6110. The substantial compliance doctrine in will execution—permitting admission of a document not strictly compliant with the witness formalities where there is clear and convincing evidence of testamentary intent—is codified at Probate Code § 6110(c)(2). This is sometimes called the harmless-error rule.

The power-of-appointment theory described in the third mediation story derives from Probate Code §§ 600 through 695, which govern the exercise of powers of appointment. Specific reference to the powerholder's intent is generally required, but California courts have on occasion applied substantial-compliance principles. The legal contest between strict and substantial compliance in this area is a live area of doctrine.

Contingency-fee arrangements in trust litigation are governed by Business and Professions Code § 6147.

Chapter Eleven: The Justice Gap

The statistic that ninety-two percent of the civil legal problems of low-income Americans receive no legal help or inadequate help is from the Legal Services Corporation's *Justice Gap Report*, most recent edition as of the book's publication. The related statistic that at least one party is unrepresented in roughly three-quarters of civil cases in state courts is drawn from research by the National Center for State Courts.

California has approximately 39 million residents. The author's practice accepts, across a fifty-year career, cases reflecting the statewide pattern described in earlier chapters. Intake volume, acceptance rate, and case-economics observations are the author's own.

Appendix: For Families

The statutory citations in the appendix are the authoritative versions as of the book's publication. California law is revised; readers should verify current text before relying on any specific provision. The general practice of consulting counsel licensed in the relevant jurisdiction, and practicing in the relevant area, is the best check against obsolescence in any printed reference.

The preservation checklist, red-flag lists, and meeting-preparation guidance reflect fifty years of observation of what helps and what does not. None of it is a substitute for legal advice tailored to the reader's facts.

A NOTE ON CITATIONS

Full case citations, in the form used above, are the standard reference format for California legal authorities. A reader who wants to pull any of them will find them in Westlaw, Lexis, or the California Courts website. A reader who wants the statutes themselves can find them at leginfo.legislature.ca.gov, which is the official source. No paywall.

Made in the USA
Coppell, TX
21 June 2026

82576887R00094